REPAIRING INTIMACY

REPAIRING INTIMACY

AN OBJECT RELATIONS APPROACH TO COUPLES THERAPY

Judith P. Siegel, Ph.D.

JASON ARONSON INC.
Northvale, New Jersey
London

Production Editor: Judith D. Cohen

This book was set in 12 point Goudy by Lind Graphics of Upper Saddle River, New Jersey, and printed and bound by Haddon Craftsmen of Scranton, Pennsylvania.

The author gratefully acknowledges permission to reprint the following:

Cover illustration: Copyright © 1992 by K. J. Bowen.

Excerpts from *"Analysis of Projective Identification: An Object Relations Approach to Marital Therapy,"* by Judith P. Siegel, in *Clinical Social Work Journal*, vol. 19, pp. 71–81. Copyright © 1991 by *Clinical Social Work Journal*. Reprinted by permission of Human Sciences Press.

Material in chapters 10 and 13 adapted with permission from *"Engaging the Couple: an Object Relations Approach to Marital Treatment,"* by Judith P. Siegel, in *Case Studies in Social Work Practice*, ed. Craig W. LeCroy. Copyright © 1992 by Wadsworth Press. Reprinted by permission of Wadsworth Press.

Library of Congress Cataloging-in-Publication Data

Siegel, Judith.
    Repairing intimacy : an object relations approach to couples
therapy / by Judith Siegel.
        p. cm.
    Includes bibliographical references and index.
    ISBN 0-87668-459-2
    1. Marital psychotherapy. 2. Object relations (Psychoanalysis)
I. Title.
    [DNLM: 1. Marital Therapy—methods. 2. Object Attachment. WM 55
S571r]
RC488.5.S5 1992
616.89'156—dc20
DNLM/DLC
for Library of Congress   92-11152

Manufactured in the United States of America. Jason Aronson Inc. offers books and cassettes. For information and catalog write to Jason Aronson Inc., 230 Livingston Street, Northvale, New Jersey 07647.

To Mitchell,
who kept me on time,
and Morris,
who kept me going

THE LIBRARY OF OBJECT RELATIONS

A SERIES OF BOOKS EDITED BY
DAVID E. SCHARFF AND JILL SAVEGE SCHARFF

Object relations theories of human interaction and development provide an expanding, increasingly useful body of theory for the understanding of individual development and pathology, for generating theories of human interaction, and for offering new avenues of treatment. They apply across the realms of human experience from the internal world of the individual to the human community, and from the clinical situation to everyday life. They inform clinical technique in every format from individual psychoanalysis and psychotherapy, through group therapy, to couple and family therapy.

The Library of Object Relations aims to introduce works that approach psychodynamic theory and therapy from an object relations point of view. It includes works from established and new writers who employ diverse aspects of British and American object relations theory in helping individuals, families, couples, and groups. It features books that stress integration of psychoanalytic approaches with marital and family therapy, as well as those centered on individual psychotherapy and psychoanalysis.

Refinding the Object and Reclaiming the Self
David E. Scharff, M.D.

Scharff Notes: A Primer of Object Relations Therapy
Jill Savege Scharff, M.D., and David E. Scharff, M.D.

Object Relations Couple Therapy
David E. Scharff, M.D., and Jill Savege Scharff, M.D.

Object Relations Family Therapy
David E. Scharff, M.D., and Jill Savege Scharff, M.D.

Projective and Introjective Identification and the Use of
the Therapist's Self
Jill Savege Scharff, M.D.

Foundations of Object Relations Family Therapy
Jill Savege Scharff, M.D., Editor

From Inner Sources: New Directions in Object
Relations Psychotherapy
N. Gregory Hamilton, M.D., Editor

Betwixt and Between: The Understanding and Treatment of
the Borderline Marriage
Charles McCormack, LCSW

Repairing Intimacy: An Object Relations Approach to
Couples Therapy
Judith Siegel, Ph.D.

Family and Couple Therapy
John Zinner, M.D.

Contents

Acknowledgment

My work with couples and families began when I was a social worker at the Hospital for Sick Children in Toronto. I had the good fortune to be supervised by Shirley Stinson, who was a pioneer in the application of family systems concepts to illness. I will be forever grateful to her for the inspiration and confidence she gave to me.

Although I had studied ego psychology and systems theory in graduate school, the two had been presented as disparate and competing approaches. It was not until I studied object relations theory with Dr. Vamık Volkan at the University of Virginia, that I began to see the linkages between the two. I am grateful to Dr. Volkan for taking time out of his busy schedule to provide me with excellent tutorial guidance. I am also grateful to Dr. Martin Schwartz, at the Virginia Commonwealth University School of Social Work, who challenged me to create theoretical connections and integrate the two theories. I am also indebted to Dr. Denny Jewart for her support and encouragement.

My years of practice and teaching in Chicago have led to rich and meaningful relationships. I would like to thank my colleagues who have continuously supported my clinical and academic development, including Drs. Judith Nelsen, William Meezan, Vicki Lasser, Don Catherall, and Michael Seiler. I am especially grateful to Dr. Seiler for his suggestions and comments on the manuscript. I would also like to thank Dr. Andrea Platt for reviewing this material.

My position at New York University has led to new colleagues and friendships. I offer my sincere gratitude to Dean Shirley Ehrenkrantz at the New York University School of Social Work for her support of this project, and to Drs. Jeffrey Seinfeld and Eda Goldstein for their ongoing encouragement. I would also like to thank Dr. Sue Simring for her comments on the final draft and Hanna Fox for her support.

Dr. David Scharff has been an involved and most helpful editor. I thank him and Dr. Jason Aronson for stimulating me to bring the case material to life and for expanding the scope of this text. I also thank Judy Cohen for excellent editorial assistance. I am most grateful to Ms. Abigail Hirschhorn and Ms. K. J. Bowen of Ammirati & Puris Inc. who enabled me to use the illustration on the front cover. I am indebted to the couples whose sessions are presented here, and trust that their identities have been sufficiently disguised to spare them any discomfort.

Lastly, I would like to thank my husband, Morris Shinderman. I relied heavily on his help in managing the technical aspects of this project, but of more importance were his optimism and encouragement. His understanding and support have sustained me and deepened our own marital bond.

Preface

Marriage therapists know all too well the consequences of ruptured intimacy. Couples who politely introduce themselves to their therapist turn abruptly on each other and attack with a vengeance. The anger and tension that flood the room pronounce the degree to which all that was once nurturing and affirming has been lost. As the therapist probes for some history and context, the juxtaposition becomes clearer. Disappointment and resentment have replaced the affection and connectedness that once existed.

It is the therapist's job to help these couples make sense of frustrated expectations and opposing needs. The idealized original state of the relationship is rarely recovered. Usually this is fortunate, for the earlier ways of relating could not possibly be sustained over time. Instead, the couple must create new ways of understanding and relating to each other. The core of their intimacy must be reconstructed.

The specific changes that are required in order to accomplish this are dictated as much by intrapsychic as interpersonal dynamics. The partners' expectations and subjective appraisals contribute extensively to the core experience of the relationship. The spouses' capacity for intimacy and the way they use each other to fulfill emotional needs are also determined by intrapsychic phenomena. Even the willingness and ability of spouses to provide each other with much-needed emotional resources and affirmation reflect the intrapsychic make-up and strength of each spouse. For these reasons, marital therapy must address individual as well as systemic dynamics.

Object relations theory provides the linkage between the subjective and external worlds and creates a theoretical framework that allows the therapist to address individual needs and perspectives. By drawing upon object relations concepts, the therapist is able to work with both the intrapsychic make-up of the partners and their ways of relating as a couple. The two worlds become connected and mutually informing, as knowledge in one area enhances the therapist's understanding of the other.

This book presents the theory and practice of marital therapy from an object relations perspective. The model outlined in this book differs somewhat from contributions of other object relations marital therapists. Object relations family therapy is constructed from different concepts that have been adapted from analytic theory. To date, the theories of Klein, Fairbairn, and Winnicott have been widely utilized. There have been, however, important contributions from the American psychoanalysts, especially Jacobson, Kernberg, Kohut, Meissner, and Volkan. The theories developed by these analysts have been extensively drawn upon in this book, and they provide theoretical concepts that allow for an enriched and expanded approach to marital therapy.

A core construct in understanding internalized object relations is the representational world (Sandler and Rosenblatt

1962). Here, the images of self and loved caretakers are stored and utilized in order to provide a foundation for the evaluation and development of all subsequent relationships. It is not possible to appreciate how relationships are created and experienced without understanding the content, structure, and functions of the representational world. In the first section of this book each dimension is explained from an analytic perspective and then expanded to explain couples' phenomena.

Part II deals with treatment issues, starting with the beginning phase. The process of engaging the couple in treatment is multifaceted, but ultimately rests on the couple's ability to commit to the process of repairing and reconstructing intimacy. Accordingly, the elements involved in the engagement process are particularized and given specific consideration.

In all of the treatment sections there is an emphasis on utilizing assessment in setting treatment goals and interventions. Successful marital treatment is often accomplished by providing stability for a relationship that is out of control and by containing any destructiveness that has weakened the couple's sense of safety and well-being. Couples with primitive internalized object relations are often best helped by learning to get their needs met in ways that are realistic and constructive. The stabilizing approach is presented in Part III.

Insight and self-discovery can also be important dimensions of marital therapy, but they are only possible when the couple's basic ways of relating have been made secure. When insight and self-awareness are realistic goals, object relations theory provides direction for the resolution of identity conflicts and projective identifications that may be negatively impacting upon the relationship. These treatment issues are also included in Part III. Part IV of the book examines termination and includes premature terminations as well as those that are planned.

The book is concluded with a presentation of treatment issues that are considered from an object relations perspective.

These include the benefits and risks of conjoint, concurrent, and collateral treatment approaches and the confluence of individual, marital, and family treatment modalities.

It is the author's hope that the clinical approach offered in this text will add to the reader's appreciation of internalized object relations and its impact upon the marital relationship. The intent has been to present assessment, not as a means of labeling pathology, but as an entry to the intrapsychic processes that must be addressed in the process of repairing intimacy.

Introduction

In *Repairing Intimacy: An Object Relations Approach to Couples Therapy*, Judith Siegel draws primarily on the American group of object relations theorists to construct an integrative view of couples therapy. Drawing on the work of Kernberg, Mahler, Pine and Bergman, Meissner, Volkan, and Sandler, she offers a unified theory of individual development that can be applied to the marital relationship. At the center of her work is the concept of the representational world, in which internal models of interaction are derived and modified from experience with external relationships. Clearly and methodically, she applies this view of individual psychology to the marital relationship. She details the structure of couples' relationships, demonstrating through pointed clinical examples how the object relations of each spouse affect the boundaries and defenses of the marital couple.

The particular strength of Judith Siegel's contribution lies in her detailed focus on the clinical process. In a series of vivid chapters, she outlines the principles of assessment and therapy. She then spells out guidelines for the initial clinical engagement with couples, for providing holding to them, and for the analysis of projective identification and countertransference. She gives details of the process of modifying splitting within the couple, empathic listening, and, particularly helpfully, the process of setting limits for couples with destructive behavior and addictions. Her discussion of the relationship between supportive or stabilizing treatment and insight-oriented treatment is a clear contribution, and her exploration of the vicissitudes of termination with couples adds a great deal to a much neglected topic.

Through Siegel's vivid, lively vignettes, which abound in this book, we can follow exactly what the therapist does, says, and often feels and thinks. We can see the links to the theory as the examples illustrate the principles involved in understanding the couple and applying therapeutic guidelines. I found the case of a lesbian couple with which she illustrates long-term, insight-oriented therapy to be particularly illuminating.

This book advances our field. It gives thoughtful recognition to a group of major proponents of object relations whose work has so far been devoted to individual development and therapy. The lessons of these theorists are applied with clarity and clinical acumen. This is a book that speaks both to the individual therapist and to the marriage and family therapist. It offers a creative synthesis of individual development and the couple's relationship, and it gives an original, creative formulation of treatment as a process aimed at stabilizing, informing, and renewing the couple. Inspired in depth by American object relations, *Repairing Intimacy* fills a gap in the clinical tradition, and brings us important new experience in the art of repairing the wounds that beset marriage.

—David E. Scharff

I

Object Relations
Theory

1 _____

Application of Object Relations Theory to Marital Treatment

The progression of intimacy is rarely smooth. Although partners are drawn together because of the affirming and enhancing resources they bring to each other, the very nature of intimacy demands that the couple possess strengths and skills in order to preserve it. The couple must develop ways of negotiating and resolving a wide range of problems that change with the passage of time. The couple is impacted by internal as well as external pressures; in addition to the strains created by shared living, the couple must balance the growth and emotional well-being of each partner. Intimacy often stimulates unresolved childhood conflicts and introduces new relationship challenges over such issues as control, dependency, trust, and self-sacrifice.

The forces that create the good will and bonding that underlie intimacy do not always provide the couple with the means to resolve the disparities and conflicts that invariably arise. Often couples must learn new ways of relating to each other and must challenge basic assumptions they hold of themselves and their partners. When couples fail to do this, the closeness and mutual commitment are ruptured. By the time a couple contacts a marital therapist, the partners have usually experienced an erosion of good feelings. The foundation of their intimacy must be repaired.

The reparation of intimacy calls for an appreciation of intrapsychic as well as interpersonal dynamics. Marital dynamics cannot be understood without recognition of how spouses perceive, interpret, and attach meaning to their interaction. Events between spouses are rarely reacted to with pure objectivity but, rather, according to the expectations and subjective, intrapsychically determined perspective of each. The spouses' capacity for intimacy and the ways in which partners are used to fill emotional needs are similarly determined by intrapsychic phenomena. For these reasons, marital therapy must address individual as well as systemic dynamics.

Object relations theory provides an explanation of the ways in which the subjective and external worlds are linked. The application of object relations concepts creates a framework that allows for simultaneous commitment to the individual and the system. By drawing upon object relations concepts, the couples therapist is able to comprehend both the intrapsychic and interpersonal. Knowledge of one area refines the therapist's understanding of the other.

Object relations concepts have been used to shape family and marital therapy for the past thirty years. Dicks (1963) noted that spouses with marital problems seemed to be unconsciously testing each other against the role models of earlier love objects with whom they had ambivalent relations. He suggests that marital tension is a consequence of mutual projection and that each spouse is perceived as being, to some degree, a previously internalized object. The notion of internalized parental figures and the importance of projection was also addressed by Skynner (1987), who drew upon Kleinian and Freudian concepts in the treatment of families and couples.

Framo (1970) expanded on many of these concepts and suggested that spouses are assigned irrational roles that are constructed from the internalized past of each spouse. These unconscious remnants replicate the dynamics from each spouse's family of origin and, in turn, are responsible for much of the conflict and symptoms that arise within a family. In order to reenact the irrational dynamics, it is necessary to provoke or elicit a specific response in the partner. Thus, the struggles that originate in the family of childhood are perpetuated in the dynamics of the marriage. A similar concept of object transference has been suggested by Walrond-Skinner (1977).

The concept of internalized family-of-origin dynamics was studied in a clinical research project headed by Zinner and Shapiro (Shapiro et al. 1977, Zinner and Shapiro 1972, 1975). Family treatment was conducted from a team perspective, and family assessments and interventions were focused on the re-emergence of internalized object relations in current family dynamics (Scharff 1989). The team defined and stressed the importance of splitting and projective identification in both family and marital dynamics. The concepts outlined in their publications remain fundamental to current object relations family treatment (Nichols 1988, Scharff 1989).

It is unclear why these theories had a relatively limited impact when they were first introduced. It would seem that the growing interest in the application of object relations theory to the treatment of individuals has contributed somewhat to the revival of object relations family therapy.

Recent contributions to the field of object relations family therapy by American therapists have expanded clinical understanding of the dynamics that link internalized and actual family relations. Slipp (1984, 1988) has presented schemata through which each family member's internalized good object, good self, bad object, and bad self form the basis of family interaction. Slipp proposes that family members unknowingly take on roles that have been projected by other family members in order to maintain the family homeostasis. The symbiotic survival pattern is perpetuated in order to ensure the survival of the family as a group, in spite of the developmental restrictions and symptoms experienced by individual family members. Slipp has also provided linkages between systemic, interpersonal, and intrapsychic levels of change, and he offers clinical interventions that reflect these multiple frameworks.

Scharff and Scharff (1987) have examined the importance of internalized object relationships from a slightly different perspective. Expanding on the theories of Fairbairn and Klein, Scharff and Scharff suggest that the parents' relationship to each other and the family's beliefs and conflicts are internalized by the children. When the grown children establish new intimate relationships, formerly repressed exciting and rejecting internalized objects are experienced and projected out. Family members also externalize and project out positive aspects of themselves and lose parts of themselves in the process. These dynamics influence the way family members relate and respond to each other's developmental and relationship needs. Scharff and Scharff have stressed the importance of the holding environment, not only in the therapy, but as a basic function of the family itself.

The Representational World

The theories presented thus far have concentrated primarily on the nature of what has been internalized and the ways in which this content is re-created in the marital relationship. It is possible, however, to expand the object relations family treatment approach by introducing analytic concepts that go beyond internalized content. The American object relations theorists have generated important concepts that deal with the structure and functions of internalized object relations. These concepts can be readily applied to marital dynamics and offer an enriched dimension to both assessment and treatment. Approaching marital dynamics from this perspective offers a comprehensive schema of the ways in which the intrapsychic and interpersonal are connected.

The best vehicle to conceptualize and utilize this perspective is the representational world (Sandler and Rosenblatt 1962). Here, the images of self and loved caretakers, or objects as they are called, are organized and stored. The structure, content, and functions of the representational world are interrelated but can be considered independently. Each domain impacts directly on specific aspects of identity and intimacy. The structure of the representational world is translated into the boundaries between spouses and is demonstrated in the couple's level of differentiation. Structure also explains depth of commitment and the degree of primitive defenses that modulate relationship intensity and stability. The content of the representational world shapes identity and contributes to distortions in how the self, spouse, and the relationship are subjectively experienced. The functions of the representational world influence the emotional demands and expectations spouses place on each other. Impairments in content and function unfold in the projective identification sequences that so often are the focal point of the couple's conflict.

Together, the structure, functions, and content of the representational world determine each spouse's subjective experience of self as well as the subjective evaluation of the marital relationship. Each spouse's capacity for dependency and trust can similarly be traced to the expectations of self and others that are encoded in internalized object relations.

The conflict, emotional pain, and ruptures in intimacy that lead couples to marital treatment are as much a property of the intrapsychic representational world as of the relationship itself. Past and present, intrapsychic and interpersonal are linked through the representational world. The therapist who is able to assess and intervene accordingly is best able to engage the couple and provide a specific and meaningful marital therapy.

2

The Content of the Representational World

The content of the representational world has a monumental role in shaping identity and the capacity for intimacy. Mental representations of self and significant objects are formed throughout life, but the earliest representations play an especially significant role in determining mental health and emotional well-being. Jacobson (1964) suggests that the earliest images of loved objects and of the physical and psychic self are constructed from memory traces of pleasurable and unpleasurable experiences and the perceptions with which they are associated. The images are created from a combination of real qualities and qualities attributed through projection and introjection (Meissner 1986a, Volkan 1976). Eventually the memory traces become condensed and form stable images or psychic constructs. Experiences of self and others are processed in reference to previously encoded representations and, in turn, add to the internally stored images. Representations may be preserved in their primitive form, modified to reflect new expe-

riences, or expanded as the individual experiences self in relation to new objects.

The Self in Relation to Others

It is important to understand that self and object representations
are created in an interpersonal context and that the content of
each is formed in reference to the other. The child experiences
him- or herself as lovable, funny, ugly, or stupid in the way that
important caretaking objects have reflected their judgment of
the child as being that way. The child who is aware of the
negative effect that he or she has on a caretaker forms not only
a representation of a rejecting object, but a self who is worthless
and also destructive (Horner 1989). Just as the self is only
experienced in relation to others, objects are experienced in
relation to the specific needs of the self at the time of the
interpersonal interaction. An infant who is peaceful will experience the caretaking object quite differently from the infant who
is hungry and discontented.

The affective flavor of the child's interaction with the caretaking objects is encoded within the representation and determines where in the intrapsychic structure the representation is
stored. In the early years of development, the self and caretaking
objects are experienced as intensely good or bad, and these two
sets of representations are stored in separate constellations.
Thus, the self and object images that are created under the
influence of the aggressive drive are distinguished from the
representations formed under the libidinal influence (Kernberg
1972, Volkan 1976). The defense mechanism of splitting maintains the subjective interpretation of self and objects as "all good"
or "all bad" (Akhtar and Byrne 1983).

Volkan (1976) stresses that it is erroneous to think of the
representational constructs as literal figures, but that there is
value in conceptualizing them in specific clusters in order to
clarify and emphasize the importance of content and structure.

The maturing child passes through distinct stages of separation-individuation that can best be understood by the corresponding changes in the representational world. Self and object representations are initially created and stored without boundaries, but in time they become distinguished and encoded as being separate. Representations that are initially polarized as all good or all bad begin to coalesce as the child is able to tolerate ambivalence. The progression of stages proposed by Jacobson, Kernberg, and Volkan will be reviewed in greater depth in Chapter 5. At this point it is sufficient to emphasize that until the child has successfully completed the separation-individuation process, the defense mechanism of splitting greatly influences the interpretation of interpersonal events and the content of the representational world that is subsequently encoded.

The Construction of Reality

The content of the representational images that are created is a blend of the real and the created as it reflects the subjective experience of actual interpersonal events. The content of a representation is also influenced by the existing stage of the child's development and the degree to which the drives and defenses are called into play (Jacobson 1964, Meissner 1986b). For example, the defense mechanism of splitting creates an internal and external world that is experienced by the child as all good or all bad. Projection leads to the attribution of qualities in objects that do not actually exist but have been perceived to be there by the child.

Rosen (1985), drawing on the work of Piaget, has elaborated on the way in which existing cognitive structures also shape and influence the child's interactions with the external world. Perception, which is an ego function, is not necessarily free from the defenses that may operate to distort reality. Even when the ego is functioning in a conflict-free way, the child is only able to interpret reality according to the internal schemata that have already been acquired. Events are first assimilated into existing mental representations. Only then can the child begin to accommodate and modify the internal structures to more closely correspond to external reality. The child has a preconceived notion of the object world that is essential to the child's predicting and making sense of the world. The initial schemata or organizing representations are crude but enable the child to interact in a meaningful way with external objects. Only after the child has used the existing representations to attach meaning can he or she begin to refine the representations in order to make full use of information that is sophisticated beyond the level of the existing representation. At this point, the representation itself must become modified and expanded to fully utilize and encompass the more specific data. As the child matures, the level of sophistication in symbols, language, and perception grows to enhance the psychic representations. The unique qualities of the material available to help the child distinguish external events can be more carefully processed, further refining the nature of the content that is encoded and stored in the representational world. A similar typology has been outlined by Stolorow and Atwood (1987).

Eagle (1987) suggests that the mental representations of self and objects create an implicit schemata or working model of life. Because these internal images form the core experience of the self and all interpersonal interactions, they become tacit knowledge and, accordingly, are rarely questioned. Eagle also speculates that because the beliefs about self and others acquired in the earliest years are processed through an autocentric orientation and primitive experiential level, they are not accessible to adult memory under normal circumstances. Thus, the content of the earliest self and object representations reflects primitive cognitive structures and is retained at an unconscious level of awareness.

The Earliest Representations

Because the presence and meaning of the earliest self and object representations have such a profound effect upon identity and adult intimacy, it is important to review their development. It is hypothesized that the earliest or most primitive self representations are formed before the boundaries between self and object are firmly established. Properties and functions of objects are fluidly incorporated into the self representations and are retained as such despite subsequent differentiation (Horner 1989). As boundaries between the self and objects become more firmly established, the properties of external objects are retained as object representations and also as introjects.

Introjects are representations that are experienced as not being the self but as belonging to the self (Meissner 1980, Volkan 1976). Introjects are representations based on the external objects the young child has been dependent upon; they operate intrapsychically to supply resources that regulate emotional well-being.

In the earliest stages of development there is not sufficient intrapsychic structure to retain a representation of an object that is significantly differentiated from self. However, as the child matures, there is an increased ability to tolerate the differentiated state. Introjects serve an important function in that they acknowledge the separateness of self from the object, but at the same time they allow for a continued connection of the self to the object (Meissner 1980). As Meissner points out, the presence of introjects suggests the child has acquired the ability to tolerate his or her separateness from the caretaking objects. At the same time, the introjects provide the means to avoid the threat of abandonment and thus facilitate further development of the separation-individuation process.

The early introjects are highly subject to drive influences and consequently become distorted versions of the actual interpersonal events. Kernberg (1987b) suggests that the level of aggression or libidinal qualities with which the introject is bestowed is related to the actual nature of the experience as well as the level of the drives that have been activated within the child during the interpersonal event. Thus, the early introjects are not accurate reflections of the child's actual interactions with caretakers, but reflect the subjective experience of the child in those specific situations. The introjects are experienced as intense versions of the objects, though the distortions or exaggerations are not perceived or appreciated by the child.

Introjects have a unique role in supplying the functions for emotional survival that are earlier supplied by loving caretakers. The functions will be discussed in greater depth in Chapter 3, but at this point it is important to understand the extent to which introjects are required to regulate emotional continuity and well-being in the absence of the external caretaking object. The introjects represent all the functions that the parents provided to ensure the physical and emotional safety of the child. As the self must always be experienced in relation to others, the introjects provide the mechanism for maintaining a sense of belonging and connectedness.

It is suggested that introjects play an especially important role in the formation of the ego ideal and the superego. In this way the introjects that are formed at this developmental stage maintain lifelong power in regulating shame, guilt, and esteem. If the formation of the superego is impaired by structural limitations and failure to relinquish splitting as the predominant defense mechanism, the introjects retain the exaggerated qualities and powers that were projected onto them when they were initially formed. The introjects that are the precursors of the superego are unusually harsh, punitive, and retaliative. For individuals who fail to complete the separation-individuation process, these primitive intense introjects are the only available source of psychic continuity.

Identification

Identification with caretaking objects plays an important role in the creation of self representations throughout the maturation process. Although object relations theorists debate the mechanics of the identification process, certain aspects of the object representations gradually become identified as actually being part of the self (Horner 1987, 1989). The child can actively model caretaking objects and can come to believe that the self possesses those attributes that were initially observed in others and imitated. Identification requires that a change occur at the level of the self representation, so that the quality is no longer perceived as being connected to the object, but as belonging entirely to the self. Identifications may occur at the conscious or unconscious level, although identity usually refers to those aspects of the self that are conscious.

The maturing child is able to take a more active role in expressing and shaping his or her identity. The self representations, which include body, gender, ethnic, racial, and cultural awareness, as well as the subjective meanings of these aspects of the self, continue to be shaped by the child's identification with primary caretakers. There is reason to believe that the child assimilates not only the awareness of self that is based on these physical properties, but the evaluation of what each attribute means to similar external objects who share those aspects of self. The child who realizes that he or she is black attaches the meaning of being black according to how the primary objects react to their own color and racial identity (Bowles 1988, Norton 1983). Similarly, a little girl forms an evaluation of what it means to be female based on her identification with her mother, who is also a girl (Bergman 1982, Chodorow 1974, Eichenbaum and Orbach 1983). Even cultural and national identifications are formed in reference to the meaning that is attached to these phenomena by the caretaking objects who share these identifications (Stein 1984).

As the child develops, there are increasing opportunities to experience the self in relation to objects other than primary caretakers and family members. Peers, teachers, media heroes, and countless others provide the child with potential sources of identification. These new objects also serve as references that expand the child's subjective evaluation of those aspects of identity that have already been established. As the child matures, peers and other objects carry increased power with which to influence and inform ongoing identifications. However, the earliest self representations are formed almost exclusively from relationships with primary caretakers and, despite subsequent modifications, have a profound influence upon identity.

The Role of Family in the Formation of Identity

Identity is strongly influenced by the way the child is perceived and responded to by caretakers and other important family members. Because perception of their offspring is influenced by their own unconscious representational worlds and intrapsychic conflicts, the parents respond to and reinforce certain traits in each child. Framo (1970) suggests that young children are highly sensitive to what their parents need them to be and accept a view of self that is strongly dictated by the parents' internalized schemata.

Richter (1974) proposes that children may fulfill specific object needs for their parents. The child may be unconsciously regarded as an object replacement of an important family member. The wish to seek continuity and perpetuation of family heritage is not necessarily pathological, but it may interfere with the child's psychological growth. As parents search for similarities that their young offspring have to themselves and extended family members, they unconsciously stress and emphasize designated personality traits and characteristics. Their desire to perpetuate the past through their offspring becomes problematic when their need to relate to the child in a certain way distorts, contradicts, or inhibits the actual qualities that the child possesses.

Richter also suggests that the child may be perceived and treated as a mirror likeness of one of the parents. The parents' perception of the child as being identical to one parent facilitates an emotional twinship that greatly inhibits healthy separation-individuation. Once again, the need to mould the child into set expectations causes identity distortions and confusion.

Richter has also proposed that a child may be used as a container for a parent's best or worst traits. By externalizing valued or devalued aspects of the self into a child, the parent and the marital system may rid themselves of unwanted qualities. The child may also be used to achieve and accomplish things that a parent has wished for but was unable to do.

It is also possible for the child's identity to be excessively shaped by the parents' need to influence the child to assume or fit into a larger family identity or myth. A family that perceives itself as being charitable, for example, will place undue emphasis on this quality and demand that the child demonstrate self-sacrificing behaviors at an unreasonable age.

The child's identity, then, is actively shaped by the demands and unconscious needs of the parents. The child responds to subtle cues and projections and accepts, or at least complies with, an identity that fulfills parental expectations.

The maturing child is influenced by the family in other subtle ways. A child may form an alliance with one parent and be further shaped by this identification. In order to preserve this bond, the child must reject any affiliation with the other parent and, in so doing, must repress those aspects of self that are like the rejected parent. Children must also identify with and yet distinguish themselves from their siblings, and they are shaped by their need to affirm or reject their likeness to other family members.

Family dynamics and values strongly influence the child's identity. Children are highly sensitive to the praise and suggestions of their caretakers and, through modeling and behavioral reinforcement, acquire behaviors and values from family members that may not have emerged in another environment. This can become detrimental to identity when the child is forced to assume unnatural characteristics in order to comply with parental expectations. Conflicting aspects of the self must then be repressed or selectively expressed in relationships outside of the family.

The Reemergence of Repressed Aspects of Identity

Throughout life, various aspects of the self may be cut off, denied, or repressed in order to perpetuate a chosen or imposed identification. Lax and colleagues (1986) suggest that these self representations have a disorganizing impact when experienced. Identity does not seem to incorporate all the representations of the self that have been encoded, but consists more selectively of those aspects of self that conform to internalized idealizations or expectations that are reinforced in ongoing external relationships. Kernberg (1985) suggests that many of these internalized, unconscious aspects of the primitive self are completely split off the adult's awareness but may become activated through adult experiences that rekindle the memory traces.

Intimacy activates self representations that are not typically experienced in other situations or interpersonal interactions. The self experience is affected not only by psychic supplies that may be given or withheld by the new object, but by a completely new experience of self. As the intimate self is created, previously dormant parts of the representational world become activated. A new identity is created as the self is experienced as a loved object, a sexual object, a loving and dependent self, and a partner in a relationship that causes the self to be redefined by others. As previously unknown or split-off aspects of the representational world are brought into awareness, each partner in the relationship must struggle to accept the emerging aspects of the intimate self.

The Intimate Self

The content of the representational world influences intimacy in many ways. As stated previously, identity is sharply altered as aspects of the representational world come into awareness. Experiencing the self as a loved object may revive infantilized desires and disappointments that have long been repressed. The experience of self as a sexual object may revive similarly repressed yearnings that may create considerable anxiety or cause a conflict with prohibitive superego introjects.

The experience of self as dependent usually provokes strong reactions, as aspects of earlier dependencies are revived. Fears of engulfment, of losing the self, or of being controlled may lead to self-protective ruptures in intimacy and increased differentiation. Similarly, the experience of self as loving evokes a sense of responsibility that may revive earlier resentment and fear of further attachment.

The act of commitment to another person changes the way an individual is regarded by family members and peers. This may create a validation of self that revives affirming representations, but may also raise fears of inadequacy as the self faces further evaluation and appraisal from others. The expectations and ego ideals that have been split off from awareness surface with surprising intensity and create self-scrutiny and careful evaluation of the new loved object. Issues of adequacy surface when the self is viewed as an extension of the object and when the object is viewed as an extension of the self.

Because the intimate self is gender specific, intimacy may revive an identification with the same-sex parent that has been previously repressed or denied. The acceptance of the role of husband, for example, creates an immediate identification with the husband in the child's family of origin. If that identification has been shunned, the reawakened identification will provoke discomfort and anxiety.

Case Illustration

Laura, at age 35, had difficulty dating and becoming involved with men. She was the only child of a successful businessman and his homemaker wife, and grew up in the suburbs of a mid-size midwestern city.

Laura's father traveled extensively in Europe and would be away for several weeks at a time. On his return he would shower his young daughter with costumes and fineries from the different European cities he had visited. Laura described her father as energetic, dashing, sophisticated, and successful. Her mother, in contrast, was described as a depressed, petty, inadequate woman. She had no talents or interests that Laura admired, and she competed with Laura for her husband's attention. She apparently felt excluded from the strong bond between her husband and her daughter, and she was sarcastic and disapproving to both.

In her apartment Laura displayed a picture of her parents that was very revealing of her relationship with them. The picture, taken at a cocktail party, showed an attractive couple, stylishly dressed, with their arms casually enfolding each other. In reality, the picture was only of Laura's father. The striking woman with waist-long raven hair was a neighbor whom Laura described as more creative and elegant than her mother could ever be.

Laura became a successful executive in the media industry. Although her business did not require foreign travel, Laura chose to vacation in France at least twice a year. She decorated her apartment and dressed herself in European designs, and she was scornful of middle-America values and life-styles.

It is obvious that Laura chose to identify with her idealized father and to reject her devalued mother. This identification worked well for Laura in business, where she emulated the worldliness that made her father successful. However, Laura was a woman and had, in fact, internalized a strong, although negative, identification of herself as her own mother. This part of Laura was experienced as inert and powerless. This incompetent, joyless presence was Laura's core experience of femininity and womanhood. Laura was terrorized by this part of herself, which came into her awareness only when she socialized with American men. Her association with European men allowed her to cathect with her own positive, grandiose self representations formed from identification with her father. In contrast, American men made her feel like her mother and threatened to revive her experience of herself as a worthless, devalued female.

Laura's representational world contained a grandiose self (her successful, accomplished self) and grandiose object representations (her father as a sophisticated, adoring caretaker). These intrapsychic representations were insulated and provided Laura with feelings of superiority and safety. As long as Laura was able to maintain the view of herself as exciting and worldly, she had a sense of well-being.

However, Laura's representational world also contained a devalued self (her unattractive, inert female self) and devalued object representations (her mother as a critical, withholding rival). Laura's experience of these parts of herself caused her to become despondent and self-abusive through eating and drinking binges. If Laura was not praised and reinforced by outsiders, she became vulnerable to experiencing the "bad" self and object representations that intensified her depression and self-directed rage.

In relationships, Laura was very prone to merger. She made rapid assessments of people, denouncing most as bourgeois and dull. Some, by merit of talent, prestige, or European association were deemed special and were assigned considerable power in regulating her self-esteem. Laura's awareness of the power others had over her added to her discomfort around intimacy. Her search for the perfect European lover ensured that she could always return to America, where she was, to her own way of thinking, self-directed and independent.

From this case example it can be seen that identity is altered by the concept of self as part of a couple and by representations that are activated by the experience of self as a lover or loved object. It also illustrates how, despite a child's wish to identify only with valued qualities of caregivers, the devalued aspects are also incorporated into the representational world. Often, it is the revival of these unacceptable aspects of the self that restrict and complicate the capacity to become intimate.

3

The Functions of the Representational World

The content of the representational world is important not only for the way in which it shapes identity, but also for the functions that the representations provide in order to preserve psychic well-being.

Winnicott (1958, 1962) has suggested that the infant is often on the verge of an unthinkable anxiety. The young child has no way of coping with anxiety without enlisting the soothing resources of a caretaking object. The comforting object supplies an important function to the child, who would have no alternative but to emotionally shut down in order to escape an overpowering emotional force.

Individuation is only possible to the extent that the child is confident in his or her own capacity to restore psychic equilibrium independently. This requires not only well-established self and object boundaries, but well-internalized introjects of the soothing object representation that will not be destroyed or split off in times of distress.

Soothing Functions

Kohut (1971, 1977) has proposed that the soothing functions are first provided by empathic selfobjects who have been able to successfully tolerate and contain anxiety and other strong emotions that have overpowered the child. The child is at first dependent upon the idealized selfobject to provide reassurance and security as needed. Later, these functions are internalized and become properties of the self (Tolpin and Kohut 1980). The child who has lacked caretakers to facilitate this, or whose own levels of anxiety and rage prevent adequate internalization of a comforting or soothing object representation, is severely compromised in his or her ability to manage anxiety and restore psychic equilibrium. The lack of self-soothing abilities impacts upon subsequent relationships with external objects, who are needed foremost for the comfort and reassurance they can potentially provide.

Esteem

Self-esteem, like self-soothing, is not inherent in the self, but is initially supplied by an idealized caretaker, who mirrors approval and worth to the child. The child looks to the selfobject for confirmation and absorbs a sense of value and importance from the responses of the selfobject. The young child is initially completely dependent upon the nurturing objects to supply resources at critical moments. Aspects of these affirming and validating experiences are internalized and become the basis of the functions supplied by the representational world to maintain psychic well-being. Only if the child is initially supplied with sufficient external approval and validation will he or she be able to independently maintain an adequate self-regard.

Kohut suggests that the quality of the mirroring and idealizing activities between the child and the nurturing objects is critical to the emotional development and formation of a healthy self.

Individuals who have never been made to feel worthwhile or secure will have a paucity of affirming self representations, object representations, or introjects to supply these needed functions. The regulation of esteem and anxiety will be needed and demanded from external objects (Schwartzman 1984). Individuals who lack internalized resources become dependent on intimate objects to supply the missing functions, and they seek to control their new love objects in the same way that a child mentally controls a selfobject. If the partner fails to provide a needed function, or refuses to be controlled, marital conflict and unhappiness ensue.

Case Illustration

Saul was almost 40 years old when he met Fran. He was attracted to her warmth, her humor, and the ease with which she related to people. In contrast, Saul was an intellectual man who was aloof and awkward in social situations. Saul had always been the favorite child of his mother, but became the hub of her existence after she became bedridden with a serious heart ailment. During his childhood Saul spent much of his free time with her and worked hard to make her proud of him. His only sibling, a sister, had bonded with their father, and after his mother died, Saul experienced a complete lack of family support. He felt excluded, devalued, and helpless, and he became progressively withdrawn and invested in intellectual pursuits.

Fran, who had initially consulted Saul for professional expertise, was flattered that a man with his status could be interested in dating her. She delighted in his intelligence and was proud of his accomplishments. In time, Saul became totally dependent on Fran's attention and praise. If she was preoccupied or not available to listen to him, he felt excluded and rejected. He was resentful of the casual friendships that Fran built so easily, and he was jealous of the small talk she would engage in with the neighbors. The situation was exacerbated after the births of their children. Saul felt left out and resentful that he could not be the central figure in her life, as he had been in his mother's. Saul had wished to re-create a merger with an affirming object who was as exclusive to him in her loyalty and devotion as his lost mother had been. Instead, he re-created the content of his representational world, through relentless demands and insatiable needs that led to a repetition of his being devalued and rejected.

4

Investing Resources in the New Object

Intimacy necessitates a reorganization of the representational world so that the new love object can be given special meaning and value. Typically this involves investing the new object with qualities and properties from the existing self and object representational world. As the lover is invested with aspects of the idealized representational world, he or she is able to take over psychic functions that were formerly conducted internally. The concept of investing in an external object implies a merger of the representational and external worlds. Once this is accomplished, the lover is empowered with the ability to regulate security, esteem, and other functions that determine emotional well-being.

The powers of internalized representations and introjects cannot be overemphasized, as they define, or at least influence, the subjective experience of relationships. Because children perceive their caretakers as omnipotent, the functions provided by primitive representations retain some of their power and magical qualities. This dimension is transferred onto the new external object, who, like the internalized object, has the power to influence and regulate emotional well-being.

To illustrate the power of the object in influencing subjective well-being, it is useful to think of a toddler who falls and scrapes a finger. The child, perceiving the caretaker as having healing and nurturing powers, runs to the external object for help. Because the child allows the caretaker to carry soothing functions, the child will accept the stronger person's reality, and if given reassurance, will experience him- or herself as healed despite the physical injury. The importance of the scraped finger and any remaining twinges of pain will be split off from awareness or minimized in order to maintain the feeling of security and well-being created by the loving object.

Intimacy creates an external object who can be endowed with functions and powers that were formerly possessed by introjects and object representations. The investment of functions allows the new object to supply feelings of safety, well-being, and esteem. The investment and acceptance of psychic functions partially explains the dependency and regression that accompany intimacy. The more the new source is needed to supply affirmation, reassurance, or other critical functions, the greater the degree of dependency. Thus, individuals who have deficiencies in the resources of the representational world will be particularly prone to excessive reliance and merger with external objects. The new objects, endowed with idealized properties, will be expected to supply the loving and nurturing resources that were originally withheld.

The new object is endowed not only with the idealized properties, but also the "bad" components of the representational world. The process of projection allows for a continuation of the self experience and also provides an important function in further establishing boundaries between the self and internalized objects (Meissner 1986b, 1987). By projecting undesirable qualities to new external objects, the self is able to establish greater distance from the qualities it seeks to reject.

The introjects of an individual who has not resolved the separation-individuation process retain the exaggerated qualities that are caused by the splitting process and its effect on perception. The primitive introjects are less available for ongoing modification and are most easily projected out into new external objects.

As Seinfeld (1990) has pointed out, intimate relationships will be experienced according to the expectations created by the content and deficiencies of the earliest internalized object relations. Projection is used in both subtle and extreme ways to guide interpretation and establish meaning in interpersonal relationships. Volkan (1976) has suggested that until the separation-individuation process has been successfully resolved, reality testing cannot be totally successful. Introjects that were based on past object relationships will intrude into the present, causing distortion or even reinvention of reality.

External objects may be invested with either positive or negative aspects of the representational world. Meissner (1986a) suggests that common themes in the representational world that may be projected involve adequacy–inferiority and victim–aggressor. Other internalized conflicts that may be externalized in intimacy involve the introjects active in the formation of the ego-ideal and punitive superego. It is also possible that the stage-specific crisis outlined by Erikson (1959) creates important introjects and representations that may be projected onto new intimate objects. Relationships would create feelings of mistrust, shame, guilt, or inferiority in either the self or the new intimate object and would replicate a conflict or poorly resolved crisis.

The specific aspects of the representational world that have been externalized and projected onto the spouse are revealed in the couple's projective identification sequences. The exact way in which the partner is induced to take on content and functions of the intrapsychic representational world will be discussed in greater detail in Chapter 13.

Case Illustration

Penny was 18 when she met and fell in love with John. He had been divorced for three years and was ten years her senior. Penny had been raised in an overprotective Catholic family and had been a quiet, respectful child who was particularly sensitive to pleasing her mother. John was outspoken, successful, and dominating. He pursued her aggressively, and they married before her graduation from college.

John was the only son of a financially struggling family that had emigrated from Poland. His mother dominated the family and totally adored her son. He could do no wrong and was pushed to be successful for the whole family.

John was proud of the sexual magnetism between himself and Penny, and he had exposed her to a wide range of sexual activities that included pornography and drugs. The couple laughed at how naive Penny had been and how much John had enjoyed corrupting her. After their first child was born, Penny began to redefine her sexual interests in a more conservative way. When she refused to participate in "old" activities, John became offended and angry. At the same time, John adored his "straight laced" wife and needed her to be respectful and dependent on him.

From the start of their relationship, Penny had needed John's approval and had allowed him to define her womanhood and sexuality in the same way that her parents and Catholic schools had defined her childhood. Penny assumed the identity John created for her, and she became involved in the social commitments John selected. John's opinion dictated her hairstyle, wardrobe selections, and even her friends. Penny was not able to disagree or express anger directly to her husband. She would extricate herself from their lovemaking by "hearing" their daughter, or avoid him entirely by sleeping in the nursery.

Penny needed John to be a demanding and critical object who could make her feel inadequate and unable to trust her own instincts. She also allowed him to carry and express her forbidden sexual and aggressive urges. Because Penny was conflicted about her sexuality, she was able to experience John simultaneously as an exciting and a punishing object.

Although John appeared to be confident and independent, he had also bestowed important object functions on his wife. John saw in Penny the good and uncontaminated parts of himself. Her acceptance and respect allowed him to believe in himself and experience himself as valuable and lovable. Penny's disapproval of him also served an important function, for despite his aggressive business transactions, which were often legally questionable, he was heralded by his mother and the business community as an upstanding community leader. Only Penny was able to denounce his "badness" and act as his externalized critical superego. The conflicts each held regarding worthiness and aggression were activated and maintained through functions each had externalized and accepted.

Control

The investment of psychic functions in love objects leads to dependency and a consequent risk of being controlled. This creates specific problems in individuals who have struggled with self-determination throughout their childhood and early adulthood. As is true for the other aspects of intimacy, the capacity to become dependent is influenced by the content and function of the representational world.

Children who have not been adequately confirmed by early selfobjects or caretakers become dependent upon idealized external objects for ongoing validation and approval. The child struggles with the need to please others, and thereby be controlled by them, versus the wish to act autonomously but still be valued (Miller 1981). The adult who has been overly controlled as a child lacks adequate internal resources to regulate self-esteem and anxiety. Intimacy becomes equated with the need to constantly please others in order to maintain the attachment. The ensuing conflict over dependency and fear of being controlled reflects a lack of trust in internalized object representations. The inability to become dependent on an object can be as problematic as excessive dependency and stems from similar deficiencies in the representational world.

The capacity to be close enough to endow objects with important psychic functions, but to remain essentially self-defined, is described by Stierlin and Weber (1989) as related individuation. Stierlin and Weber suggest that individuation involves the ability to know oneself, establish and pursue self-serving goals, and to take full responsibility for all aspects of self. The "related" component to this dynamic is the capacity to stay meaningfully connected to significant others and is as important as the ability to individuate.

Related individuation is the product of a representational world that provides internalized objects that are sufficiently responsive and affirming to allow trust and intimacy to be generated. It is a product of a self that is capable of managing anxiety and self-doubts and has experienced love as an affirmation rather than as a loss.

Case Illustration

Scott was the younger of two sons born to a financially successful businessman. Scott's father was described as a competent, outgoing man who dominated everyone in a subtle but firm way. Scott's mother was infantilized or ignored by her husband, and she was not successful in developing a bond with Scott or his brother, as both had rejected her in order to win their father's favor.

Scott competed intensely with his elder brother, and he enjoyed demonstrating his superiority scholastically and athletically. Scott's father rewarded his younger son, who was eventually asked to join and take over the family business. The two men idealized each other and excluded all others from their distinguished fraternity.

Scott met Barbara at a health club. He was attracted to her physical beauty and her aloof attitude toward him. Scott was pleased that Barbara knew nothing about his financial success and that she was reacting to him rather than to his possessions. After their first date, Scott decided to bring Barbara into his life. He moved her and her two children into a townhouse that adjoined his. In this way, Scott could see Barbara as much as he wanted, but he could escape to the privacy of his own home whenever he wished.

Scott needed Barbara to admire him and to depend on his generosity. When she was passive and adoring of him, he could feel protective and caring toward her, allowing himself to experience vicariously the feelings of nurturance and dependency that he was not allowed to expose in his own family of origin. Scott could act as the loving object to a woman who was experienced as a helpless, needy self. However, when Barbara made any demands, she was experienced as a never-satisfied, relentless bad object—the parts of his own father he could not bear to recognize. Scott would withdraw abruptly from the relationship, leaving Barbara to feel worthless and abandoned. Scott would reinvest his energy in his business and draw upon his father's approval of his latest business accomplishments for regulation of esteem and security. By reversing Barbara's importance to him, Scott could disengage himself completely from her. Scott refused to become dependent and to lose further control over the regulation of his psychic well-being.

Scott's detachment from Barbara illustrates a lack of trust in external and internal object representations. Scott had initially turned to Barbara to affirm his true self, one that was not conditionally loved according to its accomplishments. Because internal object representations were experienced as demanding and conditional in their affection, the same was expected in external objects. Scott's experiences with demanding, controlling objects strengthened his determination for self-sufficiency.

5

The Structure of the Representational World

The representational world is defined not only by its content and functions, but by its structure. The boundaries that distinguish self from object representations strongly influence the individual's capacity for intimacy. The defense mechanisms that work to maintain the structure of the representational world come to life in the marital relationship and provide another important linkage between the intrapsychic and interpersonal.

The representational world develops and evolves throughout life, but the foundation or basic structure is formed in childhood. Jacobson (1964) proposed that the structure develops in stages that correspond to the stages of separation-individuation outlined by Mahler (1975). (See Figure 5–1.) Each stage consists of self and object representations in various degrees of differentiation, organized around the two distinct poles of contentment ("all good") versus frustration or rage ("all bad"). The defense mechanism of splitting serves to separate and protect

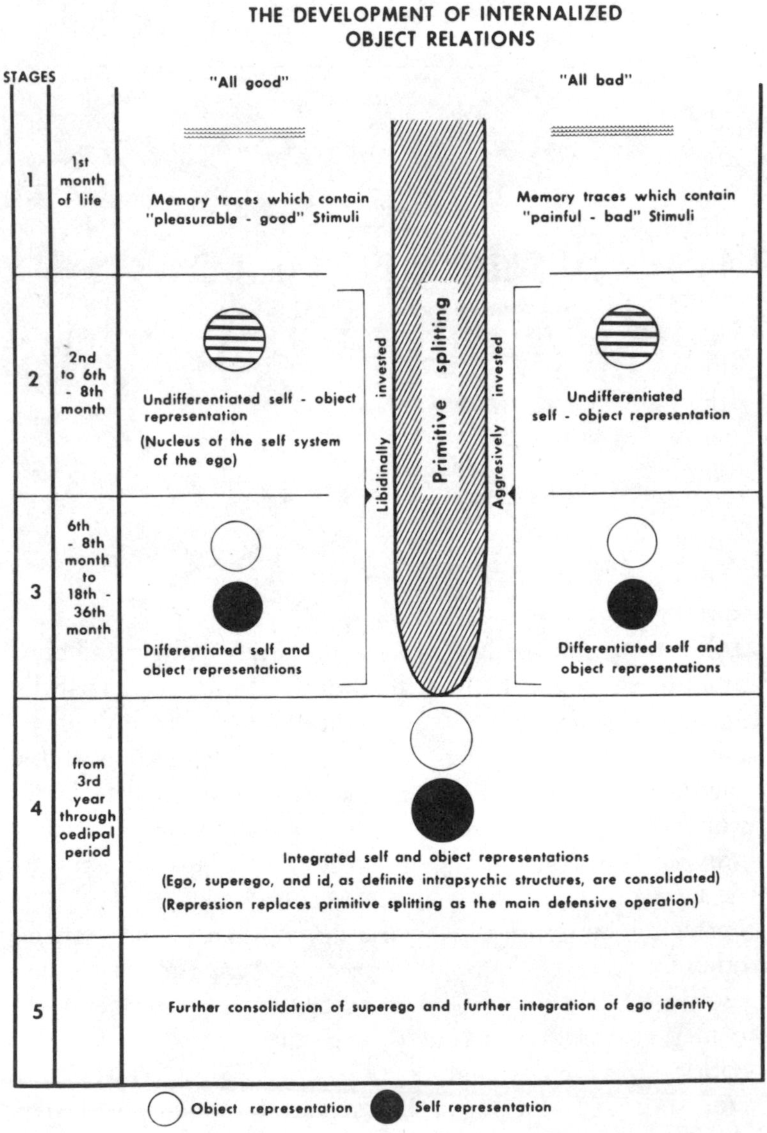

FIGURE 5-1: From *Object and Self: A Developmental Approach*, edited by Saul Tuttman, Carol Kaye, and Muriel Zimmerman, figure by Vamık Volkan. Copyright © 1981 by International Universities Press, Inc. Reprinted by permission of International Universities Press and Vamık Volkan.

good representations from bad. In order to progress into a more mature level of object relatedness, a specific structural change is required. The change in structure allows for modification of self and object representations, which in turn allows for further structural development (Volkan 1976).

The reasons that representations are encoded as all good or all bad can only be speculated. Research on infants suggests that there is a range of moods and affective states, even though these become more complex as the child matures (Stern 1985). Kernberg (1987b) suggests that only the "peak" affective states are sufficiently intense to create memorable experiences, and thus it is the intensity of the experience that lends itself to the subsequent formation of the representation. It is also possible that a wide range of experiences are, in fact, encoded in the representational world but that only the extreme representations play a critical role in psychic development. The formation of the superego and ego ideal requires that the most extreme, polarized representations be reorganized into a separate tier (the superego), leaving the more moderate representations more accessible for ongoing reality-based modifications (Jacobson 1964).

The changes in structure of the representational world follow a predictable pattern that is sequenced in stages. The stages outlined by Jacobson and Kernberg are similar to those proposed by Mahler (1975) in her observations of the separation-individuation process. It is hypothesized that the resolution of the rapprochement subphase requires a reorganization of the representational world, which leads to a more clearly defined, independent self (Meissner 1980). The issues that must be resolved at the completion of rapprochement include the ability to merge the good and bad qualities of the representational world. The successful outcome is self constancy and object constancy, which are critical to the evolution toward mature love and object relations. The structures that may be passed through along the way to self and object constancy are only pathological when the nature of the representations prevents further evolution and development.

The Schizoid Structure

Although there is debate as to whether the infant is ever completely undifferentiated from its caretaking objects (Stern 1985), the initial boundaries that distinguish self from objects are not opaque or constantly in place. The first challenge to the development of the representational world involves the establishment of distinct boundaries between self and object representations. Ray (1986) suggests that failure to complete these boundaries in the representational world creates problems with evocative memory and reality constancy. Because the nurturing object can be neither retained nor recalled intrapsychically, the child becomes dependent on the proximity of external objects to preserve identity and self continuity. However, the fear of self-dissolution is heightened by the proximity of an object that is perceived as potentially engulfing. Anxiety leads to further self-dissolution and an intense ambivalence toward the external object. Volkan (1976) defines this stage of internalized object relatedness as the schizoid structure. Structure refers specifically to the form and organization of the representational world and the degree of differentiation between self and object representations. The child who passes through this stage of object relatedness is able to create boundaries that allow for the experience of self as separate and independent from objects. Fixation at this level of intrapsychic structural development creates complications in identity and in interpersonal relationships.

The structure of the representational world governs actual relationships with external objects. Poorly distinguished boundaries in the representational world create confusion and lack of differentiation in the relationship between spouses. Related individuation becomes almost impossible to establish and maintain, as the self is constantly threatened with total surrender to the object. In a marriage where the boundaries between spouses are not secure, each spouse struggles to negotiate and take responsibility for personal needs.

Poorly differentiated self and object representations become too easily interchanged on an experiential level. Thus, a bad feeling about the object quickly leads to a bad feeling about the self. Conflict threatens personal as well as dyadic security, as destruction of the bad object would lead to destruction of the self. As a result, anger that might be felt toward the spouse must be redirected in order to preserve the security of the dyad. Because conflict must be avoided at all cost, emotions are judged to be dangerous and are shunted or split off from awareness. The lack of well-defined soothing introjects also causes anxiety to be quickly aroused and intensely experienced.

Case Illustration

Kathleen, age 35, had been hospitalized annually for psychotic episodes and depression since she was 19 years old. At age 17 she had married Graham, a religious man eight years her senior. Graham was rigid, controlling, and emotionally aloof from his wife. Outside of his marriage he had difficulty maintaining esteem.

Kathleen had steadily gained weight over the years, and her obesity added to her low self-image. She had trouble managing the home and was not emotionally available to Graham and their three children. Kathleen felt neglected and devalued, and she would spend most of the day fantasizing about being taken care of. Her feelings of disappointment and resentment at her husband's depreciative attitude toward her would confuse her, and she felt that she was both a victim and the perpetrator of her unhappiness. She was unable to distinguish the bad, neglecting objects from the destructive and helpless self representations. When her distress became unbearable, she would masturbate violently with a Coke bottle. Her attempt at gratification was also an act of self-punishment.

Kathleen's feelings were confusing to her because of the lack of clarity in the boundaries between her self and object representations. Her avoidance of conflict, her self-abusive behavior, and her excessive fantasy life of idealized objects completely under her control reflect a disturbed, schizoid representational structure. Kathleen's masochism also illustrates the concept of pain in the service of maintaining a self representation under the threat of dissolution (Stolorow 1975).

The Borderline Position

Jacobson's (1964) second stage of object relations development demonstrates a major structural change in that self representations are clearly distinguished from object representations. However, representations remain polarized as all good or all bad and are separated by the defense mechanism of splitting. Individuals who are fixated in this stage of object relatedness continue to split their experiences of self and others in all-or-nothing ways. Kernberg (1975, 1987b) has suggested that the structure defined by splitting allows the idealized representations of self and objects to be protected from the rage possessed by the bad representations.

Under normal circumstances the child is able to end the need to separate good from bad and can achieve constancy of self and object representations. The ability to merge good with bad suggests that the good representations are sufficiently strong to contain the bad representations and the accompanying aggression (Volkan 1981). Thus, individuals who become fixated in the borderline structure possess representational worlds that are dominated by neglecting and abusive bad objects. Because the good self representations are not strong or sufficiently developed, the individual experiences him- or herself as inadequate and helpless. Because the self representations are not integrated, there is diffusion and lack of identity. The lack of good, soothing, and affirming object representations creates an inability to self-soothe, and the individual must seek security and affirmation from new external objects. The borderline individual evaluates all experiences with external objects in polarized ways, so that the new object is perceived as all good when he or she is able to gratify and supply the needed psychic functions, but as all bad when there is failure of empathy or responsiveness. In this way, the internal structure dictates the cycle of relationships that always fail, adding to the mistrust and ongoing need of potentially loving external objects.

In intimate relationships, the borderline spouse relies on the partner for soothing and continuity of experience. Because the borderline spouse has such intense needs for safety and affirmation, there is often an attempt to merge with or possess the partner. When the relationship is going well, the need to preserve dyadic security often leads to triangulation of others into the relationship. When this is accomplished, any conflict or disappointment that stems from the relationship can be directed onto a third party in order to preserve the "goodness" of the spouse and the marriage. The triangled object is frequently a child, but it may also be a common enemy, including the marital therapist (Schwoeri and Schwoeri 1981, 1982).

Because of the lack of differentiation, the excessive splitting, and rampant projective identifications in borderline families, spouses may become disenchanted and enraged by their partners' faults (Goldstein 1990). It is not uncommon in such relationships for either or both spouses to become reenmeshed with his or her family of origin (Everett et al. 1989). In this case, the partner is no longer required to regulate psychic well-being, and the couple is more likely to experience intense conflict.

The lack of internalized soothing resources that is the hallmark of the borderline structure also contributes to poor impulse control and low frustration tolerance. Because the spouses are limited in their ability to soothe each other, anxiety and distress cannot be contained and are more likely to be acted out. Comfort may be sought through indiscriminate eating, drug use, or sex, which often leads to further distress and chaos.

Case Illustration

Rose and Tom, each in their mid-fifties, had been romantically involved for three years before they married. Rose worked as Tom's secretary before the affair started, and she threatened to kill herself if he did not divorce his wife and marry her. Rose was an assertive and outspoken woman, in contrast to Tom, who was meek-mannered and anxious to please others. Rose, who was considerably overweight, blamed her overeating and excessive drinking on "bad nerves," which she felt were caused by the failure of Tom's children and former friends to accept her as his wife. Rose became jealous and rageful when Tom made plans to see his two adult daughters. Rose felt excluded but refused to join them, as she perceived the children as being antagonistic toward her.

Tom's first marriage had been to a self-sufficient woman who devalued him. He was attracted to Rose because she was so "alive with feelings" and because her possessiveness made him feel important. He also felt that taking care of Rose and keeping her calm and happy gave him a purpose in life that he had not had since his daughters left home. Though Rose was prone to anger and temper outbursts, Tom tolerated these well as long as they were directed at other people.

The couple's problems centered around Tom's refusal to stop seeing his daughters. On one occasion, Rose took an overdose of Valium while Tom was dining with his daughters, and she threatened to repeat her suicide attempts unless he took her side against his family.

Rose demonstrated many characteristics of a person with a borderline representational world. Her need to possess and control her spouse is typical, as is her tendency to judge people as being on her side or against her. Rose's desperation and suicide risk reflect poor judgment and her inability to tolerate even temporary separation from her much-needed external object.

Narcissistic Vulnerability

Jacobson (1964) and Volkan (1976) have described a third intrapsychic structure that, like the borderline structure, is constructed around the defense mechanism of splitting. However, whereas the self representations in the borderline structure are fragmented, the narcissistic structure has a distinct self. (See Figure 5-2.)

This self structure consists of grandiose self representations, idealized object representations, and real aspects of the self that fulfill the grandiose expectations. These idealized and glorified representations comprise the grandiose self, which is an integrated unit. The imperfect aspects of the real self and the devalued self and objects representation form a second unit, which is split off the grandiose self. In order to maintain intrapsychic well-being, splitting must be preserved so that the devalued representations can be prevented from contaminating the grandiose self. Like the borderline, the narcissistic self can only be experienced as superior (all good) or as worthless (all bad). The feeling states accompanying both states are intense, as they are dictated by primitive introjects.

Relationships with external objects mirror the inner structure. In order to maintain a sense of superiority, the narcissistically vulnerable individual needs to be validated by external sources. The vulnerable individual is attracted to new objects who will provide adoration and verification, but he or she easily becomes critical and displeased with these objects. If the new object is highly regarded or idealized, it is likely that envy and competition will be created. The narcissistically vulnerable individual's only hope for intimacy is to merge his or her grandiose identity into a new narcissistic dyadic unit (Solomon 1989). In order to maintain this precarious unit, each spouse must verify the partner's worthiness, while at the same time upholding his or her own grandiose performance. If either of the spouses begins to criticize the other or fails to live up to the partner's expectations, the unit ceases to be experienced as all good. Because the couple cannot readily reestablish equilibrium, the relationship and the spouse become quickly devalued. Cycles are repeated where partners feel close and content with their relationship, only to quickly spiral downward into episodes of hatred and despair.

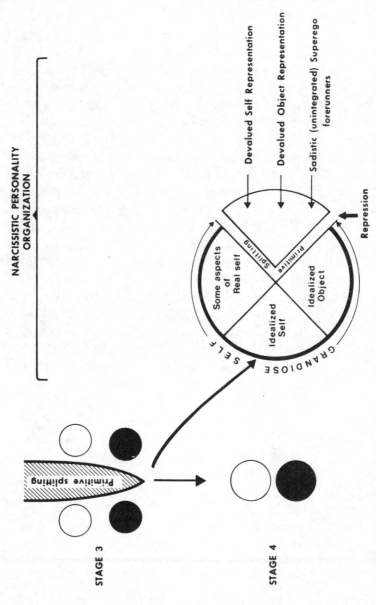

FIGURE 5-2: From *Object and Self: A Developmental Approach*, edited by Saul Tuttman, Carol Kaye, and Muriel Zimmerman, figure by Vamik Volkan. Copyright © 1981 by International Universities Press, Inc. Reprinted by permission of International Universities Press and Vamk Volkan.

The inability to tolerate criticism, the rapid reversal of well-being into despair, and the need to blame in an effort to restore narcissistic equilibrium are common features of these relationships (Lansky 1981a, Siegel 1992).

Case Illustration

Jeanne and Don were referred for marital therapy three months after their wedding. Jeanne had been in individual treatment for five years, and her therapist suggested that marital treatment might be more relevant and helpful to her at this point in her life.

Jeanne was the eldest of a sibship of seven. She had tried to win her father's approval for years, and although this had been somewhat modified after years of individual therapy, his opinion remained important to her. Jeanne's father was described as sociable and accomplished. He was also an excessive social drinker. Jeanne remembered being taken to bars and expensive restaurants for private "father–daughter" talks, and being impressed with his stories of luxury and success. Jeanne had clearly displaced her mother and competed with her sisters for her father's sole adoration.

Jeanne had a mutually demeaning and hostile relationship with her mother, who also drank excessively. Jeanne's mother was easily excitable and went through life from one crisis to another. Jeanne remembered being described by her mother as a disturbed, uncontrollable child. Each evening her father would be told exactly what the "monster" daughter had done that day to hurt and distress her mother.

The family was represented to the neighbors and extended family as a "perfect" family, and if there were problems, the children were expected to resolve them on their own. Jeanne's mother was especially intolerant of her children's weaknesses and would often humiliate Jeanne with sarcastic reminders and references to things that were not done in the expected style.

Don was the youngest of three children. His mother had come from a relatively affluent family, and she had been well educated as a young woman. She had married "beneath" her family's social and financial status and was forced to work as a librarian in order to maintain the family's life-style. As the years went by, she had become increasingly bitter about her marriage, and she was openly disappointed and disapproving toward her husband. She frequently drank to excess and would become attacking and rageful toward her husband and her sons.

Don's father was a quiet man who was emotionally cut off and distant. He died when Don had just finished college, and Don had few memories of spending time with him.

The couple met at a luxurious convention resort. Each was successful, articulate, attractive, and, although in their late thirties, romantically uninvolved. Don fell instantly in love with Jeanne and was unconditional in his total adoration of her. Where he was hesitant, she was brazen. Where he felt socially uninformed or behind the times, she was a pioneer in everything that was "happening." Where he was quiet and easygoing, she was emotionally vibrant and confronting. They started living together after two months of dating and were married within the year.

Although Jeanne was concerned about Don's lack of emotional awareness and his tendency toward superficiality, she convinced herself that marriage was the right decision. Her parents had made her feel like a failure for being single, and she was concerned about having children before she was too old. Don fit perfectly into her family, and her father was particularly proud and excited about a son-in-law who shared so many of his interests. Jeanne was also surprised by Don's total acceptance of her, and she had never before experienced a relationship that would not be destroyed, no matter what she did. Jeanne's temper, demands, and harassment of Don seemed hardly to bother him, and he was always available to make up and get close again.

The more Jeanne criticized Don, the more passive and withdrawn he would become. When things became intolerable for him, he would shut down emotionally and would appear to be calm but detached. Jeanne initially had thought this was a strength, but when she recognized it as a sign of weakness, she became totally contemptuous. Don rarely set limits or fought back, but retaliated with passive–aggressive habits. For example, he would forget things that Jeanne asked him to do and would have no recall of conversations that had been very important to her. Don would also spend long hours at work, which Jeanne experienced as a personal rejection.

When the couple socialized, both Don and Jeanne would be completely happy. They enjoyed each other's company and felt special and lucky to have each other. This was reinforced by other couples, who clearly enjoyed being with them as a couple. Don and Jeanne's awareness of other couples' shortcomings, and the degree to which they were heralded as the "perfect couple" by friends and family affirmed their sense of commitment to each other.

As long as Don was attentive and compliant, Jeanne was extremely satisfied with the relationship. She dreamed about starting a family and how gifted the children would be. When Don disappointed her or "tuned out," Jeanne would become enraged. She would experience Don as despicable and as unworthy of her. She felt imprisoned by the marriage and would make plans to leave him.

Don was devastated by Jeanne's threats to end the marriage, and he minimized them in order to diminish his anxiety. Jeanne's contempt resonated with his bad self and object representations. Despite his good looks, intelligence, and athletic skills, he believed that Jeanne was right to devalue him. Her criticism and rage were a familiar repetition of his mother's alcoholic outbursts, and he strongly identified with his powerless father.

At the same time, Don was deeply invested in Jeanne's grandiosity. It was only because he saw her as being perfect that he could allow her to demand and devalue. She carried the entitlement and expectations for both of them, and he could allow her to define him and regulate his self-worth instead of carrying this function for himself.

Through this relationship both Jeanne and Don experienced their grandiose and devalued representations. Even when the relationship was painful and out of control, it provided a necessary perpetuation of the representational world.

Self and Object Constancy

If the child develops in a normal and predictable way, the intrapsychic structure progresses to a more mature stage sometime during the rapprochement crisis. In order to have reached that point, the self and object representations become clearly distinguished from each other, and differentiation between self and object is readily accomplished. The structural challenge that is required to pass beyond the borderline or narcissistic structure is the ability to mend the split that has separated good from bad (Kernberg 1972, Volkan 1976).

Self-Constancy

Self-constancy refers to a realistic concept of self where there is integration and acceptance of a full range of attributes and qualities. The best and the worst can coexist without threatening or diminishing the capacity of the self to maintain esteem and function without excessive anxiety. This level of integration is only possible when the representational world is no longer organized around the defense mechanism of splitting. Since the splitting originally existed to protect the good-enough representations from the rage and destructiveness of bad representations and introjects, it can be assumed that there is a predominance of the libidinal (all good) over the aggressive (all bad) (White 1986).

Kernberg (1975) has stressed the importance of integrated self-images in the development of optimal mental health and mature interpersonal relationships. Self-constancy is closely connected to the individual's ability to regulate self-esteem, as the borderline and narcissistic structures create dependency on idealized objects or upon unrealistic demands for external validation. It is only when self-constancy is reached that the individual is able to "feel himself at the center of his own life" (Bromberg 1986, p. 439). Self-constancy is therefore a prerequisite for healthy interpersonal relationships. The demands placed upon self and others must be attainable without the employment of primitive defenses, such as projection and denial. Healthy related individuation to a loved object can only be achieved when the object can be approached in a realistic way with the reality-based resources only available to an integrated self.

Object Constancy

The process of attaining object constancy is similar to the steps involved in the acquisition of self-constancy. It is assumed that object representations and introjects are experienced as being distinct from the self. The challenge is to allow integration so that the best and worst aspects of a representation can be allowed to exist simultaneously.

The psychological and interpersonal consequences of integration are quite profound. Kernberg suggests that the primitive, fantastic, and sadistic images are used to form the superego and the ego ideal (Kernberg 1972). This leads to a re-formation of the psychic structure so that ultimately aggression is better contained, and ongoing relationships are experienced in a more realistic fashion.

The ability to integrate the satisfying with the frustrating qualities of object representations leads to healthier relationships and improved regulation of psychic well-being. The most definitive element of object constancy is "the capacity to retain attachment even though the object is no longer satisfactory or apparent" (Ray 1986, p. 235). When this has been accomplished, loving and affirming introjects, which are drawn upon to regulate psychic well-being, are available on an ongoing basis. The individual who has reached object constancy is able to maintain a connection to these vital resources, even in times when that object is experienced as failing or neglecting. Whereas an individual with a borderline or narcissistic structure cannot access the good introjects in moments of dysphoria, the individual who has reached object constancy can maintain an unbroken connection to the loving and soothing qualities possessed by an object that may be momentarily experienced as frustrating. Ray speculates that the capacity to maintain this stable connection is required before the object can ever be valued beyond its role in satisfying needs. This capacity is thus a prerequisite for genuine empathy. Only the integrated self is able to tolerate a wide range of responses from the loved object without relinquishing the attachment. Only the integrated self is capable of loving the object independent from the functions it provides.

6

Boundaries in the Marital Relationship

The structure of the representational world determines the extent of splitting in intimate relationships and the boundaries that will maintain individuation within the marriage. Boundaries exist to define the degree of differentiation each spouse has from the other and to define the couple as a system distinct from other external objects. As Hamilton (1988) has pointed out, external objects may be defined to include extended family, work, friends, pets, or even inanimate objects.

The boundary between spouses reflects the degree to which each has invested psychic properties in the other and is dependent on the partner to maintain personal well-being. A spouse who has relegated esteem and soothing functions to a partner usually has a stronger couple than individual identity. The "other half" is often idealized, and every attempt is made to preserve the cohesion of the good unit. It is not uncommon for partners to deny and reconstruct reality in order to avoid conflict that might lead to rejection or abandonment.

Boundaries also indicate the degree to which the spouse is regarded as an extension of the self versus a distinct individual in his or her own right. If self and object representations are easily confused within the representational world, there will be a tendency toward merger with intimate objects in real relationships. In the schizoid structure, the threat of dissolution of distinct self-representations may activate behavior that attempts to protect the self from the threats inherent in intimacy. Aloof, impersonal behavior often serves a defensive function as it maintains the distance required to preserve a fragile sense of separateness. In spouses with borderline structures, the beloved partner is experienced as the all good, nurturing object. Possession of the object is required in order to guarantee protection from the internalized bad object world and to provide continuity of pleasurable experiences. A similar kind of merger can be found in relationships that reflect a narcissistic structure, for the beloved object must be accepted as part of the grandiose self, where it can best be regulated. Thus, the spouse is experienced as existing only in relation to the self, and intimacy must be regulated in the way that safeguards and preserves emotional well-being.

The boundaries that exist between the couple and external objects similarly reflect the inner representational world. The external boundary indicates the degree to which partners need and allow each other to establish meaningful relationships with objects outside of the marriage. Couples who are enmeshed tend to be threatened by a spouse's interest in outsiders, and often attempt to cut off interests and commitments that arouse feelings of competition and insecurity. Once again, in the subjective world, influenced by the primitive defense mechanisms, reality may be distorted in order to preserve an illusion that gratifies attachment needs and defers anxiety.

Individuals who have difficulty regulating self-esteem and who have struggled against possessive objects in their past often have a need to maintain a series of ongoing relationships and interests outside of the marriage. Multiple interests protect esteem from being excessively injured from a failure in any one area and present a range of opportunities for self-worth to be restored. Competing objects create affirmation of one's value and provide avenues of escaping domination and dependency.

Boundaries between the couple and external objects are often a source of relationship tension and conflict. Spouses who have deficiencies in internalized object relations are particularly prone to intense emotional reactivity, and their partners' availability and demands are experienced as repetitions of earlier internalized trauma.

Case Illustration

Carly and Robert had fallen in love quickly and devoted themselves to their relationship, which was perceived by both as the best thing that had ever happened to them. Without Carly, Robert felt out of control, tense, and anxious. Without Robert, Carly felt helpless, worthless, and inadequate.

The couple made love at least daily and spoke to each other on the telephone throughout the day. Robert was more outgoing than Carly and had maintained involvement with a group of childhood friends. He was also committed to his work and was obsessed with maintaining his physique through weight lifting and marathon running.

Carly allowed Robert to involve himself in his work as long as she was not with him. If, however, he needed to take a work-related telephone call at home, she would talk to him simultaneously, to the point of distraction, or find some crisis to interrupt the phone call. Carly valued Robert's devotion to exercise and accepted it by integrating it into their shared experience. She insisted on driving Robert to his running meets, and she participated in his interests by researching new exercise equipment and the latest trends in marathon running. In Carly's subjective experience, the two ran together, as if one.

Carly restricted Robert's involvement with his childhood friends and found a reason to dislike each one's spouse. However, once a year the men went on a camping trip. Robert would not sacrifice this annual event, and in order to escape further conflict, Carly developed a reaction formation and bragged about Robert's trip in order to present herself as a flexible and independent wife.

7

Splitting and Marital Stability

Splitting serves to protect nurturing representations from the rage and destruction possessed by the bad self and object representations. According to Jacobson (1964) and Kernberg (1975), the presence of splitting in the structure of the representational world distinguishes the primitive from the more mature structures of object relatedness. As long as representations of self and objects are polarized into "all good" and "all bad" spheres, there is no access to stabilizing and soothing functions in moments of anxiety or dysphoria (Akhtar and Byrne 1983).

Self constancy results from the merger of the good and bad representations into a single coalesced unit that contains modified aspects of each. The result is a representation that is open to ongoing modification based on real experiences and a cohesive sense of self that is not founded on grossly idealized and devalued remnants of early childhood.

Similarly, object constancy is a result of the assimilation of good and bad object representations into a reference system of others that is less than perfect, but consistently good enough. Analysts have suggested that self and object constancy is the hallmark of mental health (Lax et al. 1986, McDevitt and Mahler 1986). The healthy representational world is one in which self and object representations have been organized as distinct units that allow self and others to be experienced as a matrix of good and bad. Frustration and anger may occur without completely erasing awareness that the same self or object is at other times, or for the most part, good enough. Without the matrix of good and bad that is achieved in self and object constancy, anger is experienced in a more primitive and intense form. Because the soothing representations cannot be called upon to help restore calm, there is no way to soften the intensity of the emotional distress. The defense mechanism of splitting activates the other primitive defense mechanisms; as a result, judgment and reality testing are often impaired (Goldstein 1984). The result is a weak or severely restricted observing ego, which further handicaps the individual's ability to integrate new information or pursue alternative solutions.

The presence of splitting in the structure of the representational world has important consequences to interpersonal relationships and identity. If the self is not perceived as having enough idealized qualities, it is experienced as all bad. Only by projecting out the badness or by denying it can a sense of worth be reestablished (Akhtar and Byrne 1983). Caretakers and significant others must fulfill grandiose expectations, or they are regarded as worthless. Since good and bad cannot be tolerated simultaneously, evidence that contradicts the polarized view must be denied. Denial, introjection, and projection serve to foster and perpetuate the splitting (Volkan 1976) and restrict the acquisition of the more adaptive defense mechanisms. The primitive defenses and the need to protect an idealized object often lead to faulty reality testing and diminished judgment. For example, an abused wife who feels vulnerable and worthless without her husband must deny evidence of his aggression toward her. Her failure to recognize that he is often destructive and violent obscures her judgment and accounts for her decision to remain in a situation that is potentially life threatening.

Splitting invariably creates chaos in interpersonal relationships, as the significant object may be perceived as perfect one moment and as despicable the next. Because the spouse can only be seen as all good or all bad, problem solving and conflict resolution become impossible. When the spouse is perceived as wonderful, there is no recollection of problems or conflict areas that need to be resolved. Similarly, when the spouse is experienced as terrible, there is no hope and no reason to try to solve the problems and conflicts that are experienced as overwhelming. Splitting also leads to extreme mood swings, as the self is viewed as wonderful or worthless, depending on external events. The rapid shifts in how the relationship is experienced and the inexplicable mood swings and attempts to regain equilibrium add to the turbulence of the relationship.

Case Illustration

Tom and Pat were in their mid-seventies and had been married 45 years. Although the couple had fought occasionally over the years, the marital relationship became intolerable for both after Tom developed severe respiratory problems that restricted his physical activity and led to his retirement. He criticized Pat for trying to boss him and wear the pants in the family. Pat was upset by Tom's temper and his inconsistent criticism. She would express her resentment by harping on every mistake Tom made in order to vindicate herself and prove that he wasn't perfect either.

When they weren't fighting, Pat and Tom acted like newlyweds. Tom called Pat a saint and offered to do anything to please her. He praised her for working so hard to keep their life running smoothly. Tom stated that Pat had always tried to give him unsolicited advice but said that he used to be able to deal with it. Tom's good health and job allowed him other sources of esteem, and he could dismiss Pat's intrusions by trivializing them. When he no longer had these outside resources, Tom felt vulnerable and powerless. Now when Pat tried to make plans or take care of a routine chore, he would experience her as making him feel inadequate and unimportant. Pat would never know if her attempts to run the house were going to be perceived as the act of a saint or an attempt to undermine Tom's power.

Tom idealized his deceased parents and thought often about their perfect marriage. He derived strength from being able to act like his father, and he needed Pat to reciprocate by playing out his mother's role. Pat's refusal would spark intense rage and resentment. Tom would be furious at Pat for not allowing him to feel like a perfect husband, and he was disgusted with himself for not being sufficiently like his idealized father.

8 ──────────────

The Couple in Context

While the couple cannot be understood without appreciation of each spouse's intrapsychic structure, historically determined intimacy needs, and specific projective identifications, it is insufficient to attempt couples treatment from this perspective alone. Each spouse is influenced and affected by very real external pressures, obligations, and socioeconomic factors. The stress of day-to-day living and the pressures that accumulate in activities outside of the marriage are important to the well-being of the dyad.

Reality-Based Stress

A spouse who has lost a job or the couple who are confronted with a relocation to a new city or eviction from their apartment are under stress that will profoundly affect the marriage. Despite the increased conflict or symptoms that reveal interpersonal or intrapsychic deficiencies, the stress cannot be reduced by focusing on the marriage alone. There are countless stressors that affect both intrapsychic and interpersonal well-being and create daily hardships that burden and drain resources needed to sustain the marital relationship.

The stressors and resources that impinge on the couple are often as important as the intrapsychic and interpersonal dynamics. In certain cases, deficiencies in the representational world and primitive defense mechanisms weaken the ego functions and contribute to or compound external hardships. In many instances, however, the stressors that the spouses are confronted with have been created by forces beyond their control. These reality-based factors should be appreciated and often must be dealt with in the therapy before the couple is able to regain sufficient energy to work on interpersonal dynamics that have been adversely affected by the stress.

Case Illustration

The Paul family, consisting of Donald (age 30), Mary (age 29), and Donald Jr. (age 2), was referred for family therapy by their physician. The parents, convinced their son was hyperactive or neurologically impaired, had consulted three pediatric neurologists, but despite reassurance, remained convinced that their son was in some way damaged. In their first session the parents were strongly focused on the details of their son's activity level, and they supplied a history of every childhood accident he had that may have led to this problem.

Although the Pauls insisted that things between them were fine, there was a noticeable strain and high level of anxiety apparent in their relationship. They criticized each other over parenting Jr., and they bickered openly over the appropriateness of Jr.'s activities. Because they felt their son had special problems, they refused to leave him with a baby-sitter and had consequently spent little time together outside of the house.

As the parents' concern over their son was explored, it became apparent that Donald and Mary were proud of Jr.'s curiosity and interest in his environment. Their anxiety seemed rooted in a fear that something bad might happen, especially if they could not control Jr.'s environment. When the therapist suggested that there might be something else going on in their lives that they couldn't control, Mary burst into tears and revealed that Donald had been diagnosed with cancer of the spleen shortly before Jr. was born. At the time they had been given little hope, and Donald's remission had surprised the physicians.

The couple avoided talking about the cancer and said that they felt they had put it behind them as best they could. Periodically, however, Mary wanted another child, and the couple would fight about it, as Donald strongly opposed that option.

Mary had transferred her fear of losing her husband into anxiety around losing her son. Donald had difficulty talking about his cancer-related feelings and fears; instead, he concentrated on protecting his family. By getting help for Jr., he was creating an easier world for Mary to manage on her own. His fear of being a burden to her in his illness and his need for a medical cure that could not be provided was displaced onto his son. The Pauls were not able to tolerate each other's fears about Donald's cancer recurring, and they avoided this area by being preoccupied with their son. By casting themselves almost entirely into their roles as mother and father, they had reduced the intimacy they once had as husband and wife. It was not possible to help them deal with their isolation and communication problems until a safe environment had been established that enabled them to share their anxiety and begin to deal with the cancer.

Cultural and Gender-Determined Roles

Marital distress is frequently caused or exacerbated by role conflict, role overload, rolelessness, and gender-determined role struggles (Hafner 1986, Tevlin and Leiblum 1983). Within the family context, each spouse assumes a set of expected behaviors and responsibilities in relation to other family members. Role refers to those behaviors that are socially and culturally trans-mitted and guide interpersonal interactions in a predictable way (Heiss 1981). A woman who is a wife may also be a mother and a daughter. The expectations placed on her to fulfill her responsibilities as mother and daughter may cause her conflict or drain her of the resources she needs to fulfill the responsibilities of wife. Rolelessness deprives an individual of opportunities to enjoy the gratifications available through specific interactions. A woman who has lost her own mother and is unable to have children may experience profound loss in response to her perceived deprivation.

Role-determined stress is compounded by different standards and expectations that are inevitably created by the different socialization experiences of the marital partners (Feldman 1982b, 1986). Husbands and wives usually have different ideals and standards with which to measure role performance, and they are often critical or confused by their spouse's differing assumptions and values.

Gender-determined roles guide the spouses in their efforts to distribute the responsibilities of shared living. Many of the existing gender-determined roles are based on values and assumptions that have been challenged by feminists but continue to influence and confine the self-actualization of each partner (Hafner 1986, Luepnitz 1988). Gender stereotypes often restrict and inhibit the spouses in their attempts to work productively together. The gender-determined expectations that each partner has of the other can easily create stress and misunderstandings. As Tevlin and Leiblum (1983) have pointed out, these roles may also be self-imposed and can be destructive to the sexual as well as the emotional dimensions of the marital relationship.

The personal and relationship expectations each spouse carries are also influenced by values and assumptions that are culturally determined (Volkan 1979). Each ethnic group has specific gender-determined role expectations that further influence marital behavior in conscious and unconscious ways (Boyd-Franklin 1989, Falicov 1992, McGoldrick 1982, McGoldrick and Preto 1984). The culturally determined role attributes of husband and wife vary considerably among different cultures and within different socioeconomic subgroups of ethnic groups.

Cohort values also influence the expectations of the intimate self and partner. Individuals form a group identity with others born in the same time span and establish group values that distinguish and differentiate them from the generations they precede (Riley 1978). The shared literature, music, and social experiences of the group at large have a profound impact on intimacy expectations and relationship values. As Swidler (1971) has pointed out, intimacy is more easily established and maintained for that cohort of individuals who view the sacrifices needed to carry out marital and parenting obligations as complementary to individual well-being and personal happiness. Spouses who emphasize or value accomplishments that can only be achieved in work or non-family-related activities will approach marital and family demands quite differently from those who define family relationships as the primary source of self-fulfillment.

Spouses are driven and conflicted by personal values and belief systems that are specific to each individual and often poorly understood. The therapist is also influenced by culturally determined values and beliefs and can be further influenced by theories that define marital treatment in ways that exclude the full range of explanations of human behavior. Students of couples treatment usually fail to appreciate the degree to which their own belief systems influence the direction of the couples treatment. Issues of social and gender-determined power and expectations come into play in every relationship (Kantor and Kupferman 1985, McGoldrick et al. 1989). The therapist's inquiry into or avoidance of certain interactions ultimately determines which dynamics are made explicit in terms of their effect on the couple's life-style and which are left to affect the relationship in unarticulated ways. Because the unarticulated assumptions and values of each spouse profoundly impact their interaction, the couples therapist should be prepared and committed to question behaviors and responses that indicate differing values and beliefs.

Case Illustration

Anita and Sal originally sought help for their 6-year-old son, but they readily agreed that there were tensions and problems in their relationship that also needed to be addressed. Anita, age 43, was the third of six children born to a fairly successful second-generation Italian family. She had been college educated and had worked as a school teacher before she married Sal. Sal, age 46, was the youngest of four children of a first-generation Italian family. Both of his parents had worked, and he had been looked after by his eldest sister, who was twelve years his senior.

Sal was a relaxed, easygoing man who expected to be treated as the "head" of his family. He was attentive and supportive of his wife and worked hard to provide her with every possible comfort for their home. Anita was more conscientious and felt pressured to be perfect at whatever commitment she undertook. When Anita invited extended family or friends for dinner, she became anxious in her attempt to ensure that every detail was in order. In contrast, Sal would approach the evening in a more relaxed way, belittling Anita's perfectionistic tendencies and arguing that people were more interested in having a good time together than whether the napkins matched. Anita assumed full responsibility for the domestic chores and she felt resentful for having to carry the entire burden.

Conflict would also emerge when the couple was faced with a decision, for they would inevitably disagree. Rather than talking out their differences, Anita would defer to her husband. If Sal's choice resulted in the slightest problem, Anita would harp on her husband's decision and insist that if they had done what she wanted, everything would be perfect. For example, when the couple decided to buy a new car, Anita started to investigate the different models and was inclined to buy a foreign station wagon. Sal took Anita to test drive an American minivan that a friend recommended. He was very pleased with the car, and after negotiating the price to his satisfaction, pressured Anita to buy the car that afternoon. Anita reluctantly agreed, but when the van had to be serviced for ignition problems three months later, she complained endlessly, insisting that a foreign model would never have caused them a day's inconvenience.

Despite her intelligence and broad range of interests, Anita would defer to her husband because she believed that to be the duty of a good wife. Anita had great difficulty challenging her husband directly, but felt more comfortable complaining later. Her values and culturally dictated expectations led her to believe that her influence was to be exerted in areas related to the house and children and that financial matters should be left to her husband. At the same time, her years of independence led her to challenge her husband's power and control, and she struggled with her need to express her wishes versus her need to be a good wife in a way that had been culturally defined.

Sal's values also reflected his gender-determined and culturally determined expectations. Sal enjoyed large family gatherings but had never participated in the preparation; he had a restricted awareness of the energy and tasks needed to organize an entertainment. He also assumed that, like his father and other role models, he should be the one to make the decisions about cars and things that men were supposed to know more about than women. He was bewildered by Anita's need to fuss over their social entertainments, and he was deeply upset by Anita's constant criticism whenever a problem arose.

When there was tension or disagreement, Anita would start to vent her feelings. Sal would be emotionally overwhelmed and would withdraw, often walking out of the room or tuning her out so that she was talking to a totally unresponsive partner. Later, Sal would try to tell Anita some amusing anecdote and initiate love-making as a way of getting close again. Anita alternated between accepting his token of reconciliation and becoming even more upset and discouraged because she felt her feelings had been dismissed as unimportant. Even in their style of resolving conflict, both spouses were governed by cultural and gender expectations they had absorbed, without challenging or fully comprehending them.

II

Practice:
The Beginning Phase

9

Engaging the Couple in Treatment

The therapist who practices marital treatment from an object relations perspective maintains a balanced interest in the intrapsychic reality of each spouse and the dynamics between the spouses. The understanding of intrapsychic and interpersonal is mutually enhancing, as the dynamics of each area are reflected in the other. Structure, content, and the functions of each spouse's internalized object relations create the subjective experience as well as the dynamics that regulate the couple as a system.

The therapist must strike a balance between intra- and interpersonal, so that observations and insights about each sphere maximize potential for meaningful interventions. The therapist must also strike a balance in focus between past and present, as the couple must be helped to identify and reorganize their ways of relating on a day-to-day basis while dealing with the remnants of the past that demand reparation.

The couple seeking marital treatment most often has no

comprehension of a representational world and little appreciation of the importance of an internalized past. Spouses tend to
focus only on their current unhappiness and blame their partner
and themselves in ways that add to the marital frustration. It is
the role of the therapist to inform the couple about the unknown parts of themselves that exacerbate marital distress and
to provide a therapeutic climate that is both safe and stimulating
enough to elicit change.

Engaging the couple in the treatment process involves
several steps that do not necessarily follow in order. The couple
needs to be able to develop sufficient trust in the therapist to
reveal private and oftentimes painful thoughts and feelings. The
couple also needs to develop some basic understanding about
the treatment process in order to establish realistic expectations
about the nature of the service the therapist will provide. As
Beavers (1985) has pointed out, the spouses must also be able to
develop some faith in the change process and become hopeful
that their relationship can be improved.

The beginning phase establishes the groundwork for treatment. In addition to creating a safe therapeutic environment,
the therapist uses the initial sessions to gather information about
the couple as a system and as individuals. This includes clarifi-
cation of the observations that are made about the couple's style
of interaction, exploration of the subjective experiences of each
spouse, and specific history that will provide information regarding the individual backgrounds and level of functioning of
each spouse. Analysis of projective identification and of the
therapist's countertransference is especially useful in generating
meaningful information for the therapist and the couple.

The therapist's early role involves seeking information for
assessment and, in the process, introducing initial elements of
change. Splitting and impulsive, destructive behavior should be
commented upon in order to better understand the history and
current level of functioning in the couple. The discussion of
these dynamics will clarify the extent of the couple's observing

ego, which is important knowledge for the therapist in planning for the work that lies ahead. Discussion of acting-out behavior will similarly test each spouse's ability to work with the therapist in taking responsibility for change. By noting and clarifying faulty communication processes, the therapist is in the same way both assessing and intervening in this aspect of the couple's relationship.

The dynamics that regulate the couple's intimacy determine, to some degree, the extent and way in which the couple is able to establish trust and become involved in the treatment. All of these factors contribute to the therapist's decision to work with the couple conjointly or concurrently.

The couple can be considered engaged in treatment when they have made a knowledgeable commitment to the process and style represented by the therapist. Whenever possible, this involves goals that can be articulated and agreed upon by all involved. The couple will have some understanding of areas that will be worked on in therapy and be prepared to work with the therapist on the affective, cognitive, and behavioral levels.

10 _____

Creating the Holding Environment

The therapist's first priority is to understand the immediate situation and to create a holding environment. This involves the ability to fully grasp and appreciate the subjective reality of each spouse. At the same time, the therapist must establish and maintain the ability to intervene in threatening or destructive interactions in order to ensure the safety of each spouse. The holding environment allows the therapist to contain the anxiety and distress that prevent the couple from working through escalating conflict (Scharff and Scharff 1991). By providing acceptance and understanding, the therapist generates soothing that was not available from the internal or interpersonal resources of the couple.

Assessment of object relatedness must begin promptly and includes observations of the couple's way of relating to each other as well as to the therapist. The level of anxiety, emotional investment in the process, and the ability to engage with the therapist are important indicators of object relatedness.

If the spouses have regressed to or are fixated in a way that suggests a schizoid, borderline, or narcissistic structure, the therapy, as well as the relationship, will be experienced in a specific way. The therapist who is able to recognize primitive dynamics early in the process is better able to respond to the couple in a way that will facilitate their engagement in the treatment process.

Couples with schizoid dynamics will relate to the therapist in an awkward, anxious way that may be masked by avoidance and withdrawal. The couple's reluctance to trust will be intensified by an invasive or overly confrontive therapist. The therapist who is able to respect the distance that the spouses need to feel safe will be less likely to threaten the couple.

Couples with borderline structures will demonstrate a tendency to vacillate in their view of the problem, their assessment of their relationship, and their commitment to treatment. Because they lack the ability to self-soothe, they will relate in a disorganized way and externalize their confusion and anxiety. The therapist who takes on the couple's chaos and projections will not be able to provide the structure and safety needed to establish a meaningful therapeutic environment.

Couples who have high levels of narcissistic vulnerability are particularly challenging to engage in treatment (Feldman 1982a, Lansky 1981a, Sharpe 1990). The therapist should be sensitive to the meaning of failure implied by the need for professional help and the couple's fear of being exposed to a potentially critical or controlling object. The therapist should also anticipate each spouse's need to protect the grandiose self in an environment where there is potential for blame and attack. In order to maintain the holding environment, the therapist must ensure that each spouse will be protected and that information will not be shared in a way that creates profound shame or retaliative rage. Control, jealousy, and confidence in the therapist's impartiality all affect the couple's ability to engage in the treatment process.

Early awareness of severe splitting, excessive mistrust, un-controlled anxiety, and/or attempts to control the session alerts the therapist to the presence of primitive internalized object relations and enables the therapist to provide the most mean-ingful holding environment. The couple's basic way of relating to each other and the therapist's initial countertransference are also important sources of information. A history of several unsuccessful therapy attempts and a tendency to recall events in all-or-nothing terms similarly should cause the therapist to proceed more cautiously until the couple has been more thor-oughly assessed.

The couple's ability to explore the relationship with both cognitive and emotional awareness is also prognostic. Limited awareness in either area may be a by-product of excessive pro-jective identifications, confused boundaries, and/or primitive defense mechanisms. Barnett (1966) has described two faulty styles of integrating emotion. In explosion, affect is spilled out instead of being digested. The individual may appear to know his or her feelings, but is actually unable to reflect upon the situation at hand. Failure to integrate the affective with the cognitive is also demonstrated during an emotional shutdown, which Barnett calls implosion. In this situation, the individual appears devoid of feelings. Focus on the intellectual realm acts to prevent and defend against anxiety and intense feelings that cannot be soothed. Both styles should alert the therapist to problems regulating esteem and anxiety that may indicate a schizoid, borderline, or narcissistic intrapsychic structure.

The therapist who recognizes these dynamics is better able to explore the subjective well-being of each spouse and to regulate the early sessions so that the holding environment can be preserved. The pace at which the therapist investigates explosive dynamics, allows conflict, and/or confronts the couple is important to the couple's ability to engage in the treatment process. Above all, the therapist must allow a holding environ-ment to develop so that each spouse feels safe. Spouses who attack each other in therapy often experience the rage and destruction in a distorted way. Frequently, the spouse who is the more rageful feels more upset after the episode. Because of primitive defense mechanisms, it is not uncommon for the angry spouse to identify strongly with the destroyed partner and blame the therapist for the destruction.

Case Illustration

Pete and Carla had interviewed three other marital therapists before they met with me. Pete, age 35, was a tall, well-groomed man who seemed somewhat withdrawn and pensive. Carla, an attractive woman in her early thirties, was more outgoing and engaging, but slightly theatrical.

As I probed into their current situation, the stress in the relationship was readily apparent. Pete had recently moved home after a month-long separation. The couple had been together four years and had been distant and unhappy for most of that time. Pete's perspective of the marriage was resigned and pessimistic. Carla's temper flared quickly, and she scorned Pete's moods and pessimism.

At the beginning of the session I tried to connect with each spouse and learn about their backgrounds and view of the present situation. Both Carla and Pete were intensely reactive to each other and would express their irritation by tapping their feet, smirking, and rolling their eyes in disagreement.

Therapist: (to Pete) You seem pessimistic to me. Can you tell me more about the way you think things are going?

Pete: I feel very close to giving up. Carla is not capable of change. She is self-centered . . .

Carla: (interrupting) Me! That's a joke! You are the one who is totally wrapped up in yourself. You walk around the place with that sad face for days. If it wasn't for me . . .

Pete: Me! How would you know anything about me? (to the therapist) What's the point?

Therapist: (interrupting) Carla! Pete! We need to slow things down here. I can tell you are both angry and I'd like to try to understand that better, but it will never happen if you two keep interrupting each other. You each have something important to tell me, and I'd like to give each of you that chance. Try to talk just to me, and I'll make sure there's plenty of time for each of you to answer.

Pete: (a few moments later in the session) We don't really have any friends now. I can't remember the last time we went out with another couple. Part of the reason is that the house doesn't look very good . . . we have old furniture, it's pretty beat up, but we have two dogs . . .

Carla: We have old furniture because we don't have any money. And the last time we went out it was for *my* business and you got so uncomfortable socializing with people who are at your boss's level that you were miserable all night!

Pete: You just don't understand.

Therapist: (to Pete) You're ready to drop this now? (Pete nods sadly in agreement) Can you try to explain more of it to me? I get the sense you have a lot of ideas and feelings that don't get expressed completely.

Pete: I guess Carla does most of the talking.

Carla: Someone has to. You can walk around the house for days with a sad face and I won't get a word from you. And if you're going to talk about something, why don't you tell it the way it is?

Pete: (to the therapist) I am telling the truth! Before I met her I used to go out all the time . . .

Carla: Well, people grow up, Pete. It's not college any more and everyone is not poor. Our house is not fit for company, and it's not just the dogs!

Therapist: There is so much anger and resentment between the two of you. It sounds like things have been building up for years, but this anger feels destructive to me right now. I see the resentment, but I also know that both of you care enough about your relationship to interview three therapists in order to make sure you get the help you need. Let's slow down together and see if we can't try to understand the anger and disagreement in a way that isn't quite this stressful.

Carla and Pete flooded the room with their tension and anger. The most important task was to establish a safe environment where the couple could be helped to establish some degree of emotional control. Because of the intense emotional reactivity of both spouses, I directed their responses to me instead of each other. I also regulated the format of the session by instructing both to hold their comments and reactions until it was his or her turn to respond.

Pete needed encouragement to express his thoughts and had difficulty processing his feelings. Carla, on the other hand, was highly reactive and quickly expressed her feelings, without always collecting her thoughts. Carla's anger was used to justify Pete's withdrawal, and both reactions were experienced as punitive and destructive.

My main concern was to establish safety for both Pete and Carla. My comments were offered in a way that was respectful rather than critical and in a way that established my concern and control of the session. Rather than rejecting their belligerent behavior, I stressed that it was important for me to get to know them thoroughly. I reinforced how important it was to me to understand their feelings, but I asked them to slow the process down so that I could use their anger in a constructive rather than a destructive way.

It is important that the therapist not lose control in the early phase of the engagement process. From the beginning of the session, Carla and Pete provoked intense countertransference in me. They interrupted each other's communications to me with dramatic facial gestures and sarcastic verbal responses, and they were scornful, impatient, and condescending. Both were initially preoccupied with their resentment and bitter feelings and could have easily turned me into a passive, helpless witness of their destructiveness. My sensitivity to their narcissistic injury and defensive postures helped me provide the acceptance and soothing that each needed. Their feelings were valued and validated, but channeled into a forum that was safe. A pace was created that allowed for depth and a better opportunity to achieve genuine understanding and expression of feelings. The session was experienced as integrative rather than explosive, and as a chance to be understood rather than condemned or defeated.

11 _____

Assessing the Couple's Commitment

An important part of the engagement process is correctly understanding each spouse's interest and commitment to repairing the relationship. Couples who are harboring deep resentment and hostility first need to renew their commitment and willingness to regain closeness. If either one of the spouses is not able or willing to work on letting go of the pain from the past, it is highly unlikely that the couple will be able to benefit from marital therapy. Spouses who cling to pain as evidence or proof that the spouse cannot be trusted again are not able to truly engage in repair of the marriage. Very often a spouse who is unable or unwilling to become involved in working on the marriage is asking for help separating or getting a divorce. It is not uncommon for a spouse to stay in a deteriorated relationship for security or retaliation. While that individual may not be ready to ask for a divorce or acknowledge the wish that the relationship was over, his or her ambivalence will prevent an honest commitment to treatment that aims to generate renewed intimacy. Because marriage therapy and divorce therapy are different in focus and modality, a marital therapist should appreciate the meaning of a spouse's lack of willingness to work on the marriage and should question his or her own role in trying to save a marriage when only one spouse is interested.

Many spouses present with intense anger and resentment. Strong feelings are not, in their own right, an indication of lack of commitment to restoring the relationship. The therapist should be aware, however, of the damaging impact of intense anger on the fragile process of renewing intimacy. Spouses often feel justified or entitled to revenge, and in their attempt to be heard, create even more resentment and misunderstanding. Often, the anger reflects the unresolved pain of a deep narcissistic injury that has not been validated or responded to. The spouse who clings to the past may be asking for some validation of his or her suffering and may need acknowledgment or reparation from the partner in order to recommit to the relationship.

Lack of commitment to the relationship is revealed by a spouse's lack of responsiveness to his or her partner and an underlying sense of detachment. If the spouse is bitter or angry, it is usually accompanied by aloof resignation. The spouse most often remains indifferent to expressions of reconciliation or tenderness from the partner. Often the therapist experiences a strong countertransference reaction of pessimism and/or powerlessness and can sense the spouse's reluctance to invest in the therapy.

If there is a strong element of resistance and lack of commitment, it is often advantageous to see each member of the couple individually. Although this raises the clinical issue of how to handle secrets that are shared with the therapist, it is imperative for the therapist to learn of any plans to end the relationship and the existence of extramarital affairs. A spouse who is investing more emotional energy in leaving the relationship than in repairing it needs individual help in sorting through his or her ambivalence. The partner's attempts to restore intimacy at this time are usually insufficient to help the spouse recommit to the marriage, and conjoint therapy that attempts to improve the relationship while ignoring the ambivalence of one partner is doomed to fail.

Case Illustration

Phyllis and Steve were in evident distress in their first session. Steve had called for the appointment because Phyllis had grown increasingly distant over the past few weeks and was hardly speaking to him at all. Steve was afraid that Phyllis was thinking about leaving him, and he was primarily upset because of his fear of losing Josh, the couple's 2-year-old son.

In the early part of the session, I was struck by Steve's expression of intense feelings and Phyllis's total detachment from Steve and me. Phyllis made no effort to defend herself against Steve's criticisms or to respond in any way to his self-beratements and apologies. I wondered if Phyllis was depressed, but my attempts to assess her mood and well-being were rebuffed.

Midway through the session I asked Steve to return to the waiting room for ten minutes so that I could speak to Phyllis in private.

Therapist: Phyllis, it seems to me that you are very distanced from Steve and don't seem to care very much what he has to say about himself or you. I don't have a very clear idea of what is going on for you right now, but I know you are not putting very much energy into this marital treatment. Can you tell me what's going on?

Phyllis: Will you tell Steve?

Therapist: No. Not unless there is physical danger involved. I will tell you whether or not I think you should tell him, and I'll tell you if I might not be able to continue working with you for very long if we disagree, but I won't reveal what you tell me.

Phyllis: I'm leaving him. (silence)

Therapist: Go on.

Phyllis: I have my plane tickets and I'm taking Josh with me. He'll never see us again.

Therapist: You seem very determined to go.

Phyllis: I can't tell you where. No one knows. I'm starting a new life. He'll never find us.

Therapist: Leaving like that is going to create all kinds of legal problems around custody and kidnapping. I can tell you want your son, but I think there must be another way of ending this marriage.

Phyllis: No. He'll take Josh. You don't know what he's like. He'll go for sole custody. I've smoked pot for years. He's going to use that against me. And he has a temper. I won't be safe unless I'm gone when he finds out.

Therapist: Phyllis, why did you come here today to talk with me?

Phyllis: He has a gun. I don't want him to kill himself. He wouldn't come here without me, but at least he'll have your number when he finds out I've left him.

Therapist: Right now I see you as being desperate. You must have some very good reasons for believing that Steve would hurt you if you tried to leave him. I'm sure he has threatened to take Josh away from you, but I don't believe that a court would let that happen just because you smoke pot. Is there something else you want to tell me?

Phyllis: No. Why do you think I wouldn't lose in court?

Therapist: I think Steve may have used this as a way of frightening you and making you feel that you have no power. If he has been violent to you by hitting you or threatening you, then a judge would see that as far worse a problem than smoking pot.

Phyllis: I never knew that.

Therapist: Would you let me help you find a lawyer who could tell you what your chances are in court? Phyllis, what you are doing by leaving like this is going to do you far more harm than good in the long run. I can help you make a plan that will keep you safe if you are afraid of Steve. Will you let me help you?

The case of Phyllis and Steve is a dramatic example of the importance of the therapist having a clear grasp of the whole situation. Few couples will present with this degree of urgency, but the therapist must be sensitive to the meaning of resistance to working on the relationship. The secret that the spouse will not tell the therapist in front of his or her partner often has important meaning to the purpose of the couple's treatment and its outcome. Concurrent sessions inevitably provide the forum in which affairs, plans to leave, and other secrets emerge. Failure to allow this information to be revealed will prevent the spouses from becoming engaged in any form of meaningful treatment. Further discussion on concurrent and conjoint sessions is offered in Chapter 21.

12 ————————————

Instilling Hope

As stated earlier, the expression of anger and pessimism does not necessarily indicate lack of interest in staying in the relationship. Many partners have been repeatedly hurt and disappointed by each other and are overwhelmed by their pain. This is exaggerated in individuals who have primitive defense mechanisms and who tend to split their experience into "all" or "nothing."

One of the therapist's primary goals in the engagement phase of treatment is to generate improved understanding between the spouses. A spouse who feels understood may begin to develop hope that the partner is capable of change. Until this happens, the injured spouse may find it impossible to believe that the situation can be improved. The therapist is often able to provide a feeling of safety and to control the pace and focus in such a way that partners are better able to express themselves and feel understood.

The skills involved in developing and enhancing empathic listening will be discussed in Chapter 16, but it is important to generate the sense of being understood early in the engagement process. Each spouse's ability to listen instead of minimize, belittle, or defend his or her own position helps the partner feel valued and responded to in the relationship. Very often, the act of being listened to and of having sensitive feelings validated is the selfobject function that was most painfully missed throughout the marital trauma. The therapist who can facilitate a clearer level of understanding between the spouses early in treatment can demonstrate the potential of therapy and can renew hope.

Case Illustration

Andrew had asked for the first available appointment, as he was afraid that his wife, Meredith, was going to leave him. The couple had been married eighteen years and had two teenage children. Meredith had discovered that Andrew was having an affair, and although he had denied it initially, she had confronted him with information she had uncovered by going through their old phone bills. Meredith was now demanding all the phone bills from Andrew's business and was constantly calling him to check up on what he was doing.

In their first session, Meredith started to cry and talk about how she just couldn't believe Andrew anymore. In a tearful, agitated state, she said that it was in her best interest to get a divorce and to try to build her life over.

Therapist: What is your response, Andrew, when Meredith talks like this?

Andrew: I am devastated. I don't want a divorce. We have two beautiful children and a beautiful home. There is no reason why this has to happen.

Meredith: Why didn't you think of that before you started fooling around?

Andrew: That is behind me! I've begged you to forgive me. I've said I'm sorry a hundred times. I don't want a divorce. You have to believe me!

Meredith: (crying and getting increasingly agitated) How can I believe you anymore? Why should I? (to the therapist) He's made a total fool of me. I told him I knew something was going on. . . . I asked him if everything was all right with us. He made me feel like I was crazy . . . inventing things . . . paranoid!

Andrew: (in a stern voice) Meredith, you make it sound like I've been doing this for so long and you've had such an unhappy life with me. We've had a damn good marriage for 18 years and this affair was nothing. It wasn't even really an affair. I was with her once, only once. I've told you a thousand times it's behind us now and we have to let it go. You can't go on this way. (As Andrew talks to Meredith, she stops crying.)

Therapist: I notice that when Andrew talks to you, Meredith, you seem to get calm. You seem to be agreeing with him. Perhaps there is a part of you that wants out and a part of you that wants to believe in Andrew.

Meredith: I feel better when he talks to me. He makes me feel like he really does love me. But when I think about him with another woman, I want to die.

Therapist: Andrew knows how to reassure you, but inside you're still upset and confused.

Meredith: (starts getting distressed again) When I start to think about it again, I get furious. I don't think I do trust him. I don't know what he's really doing. Everyone loves him—it's easy for him to do exactly what he wants. I won't know unless I check on him all the time, but what kind of life is that for me—always thinking he is with someone.

Andrew: (interrupting in a patronizing voice) How can you say those things about me? Look how upset I've been the past few days. You've made my life miserable. You cannot keep on checking on me. I've never cheated on you before, and I told you I never would again.

Therapist: (interrupting) Andrew, I know it's important to you that Meredith let go of her anger, but I think you're leaving out one thing that might help. I'm not sure you have really understood what

Meredith is trying to say right now, and I think it is very important to her that for now you just try to understand her experience.

Andrew: (to therapist) She is just overreacting to this whole thing. She is totally out of control . . . not thinking clearly.

Therapist: (to Andrew) You feel that she is being too hard on you, and it makes it difficult to hear everything that she is saying.

Andrew: I understand her.

Therapist: I'm not sure you're right about that. Why don't you check it out?

Andrew: (reluctantly) You're afraid I'm going to cheat on you, right? Even though I've told you a hundred times this will not happen again. I'm a very busy man. I can't have you checking on me every five minutes. This is craziness.

Therapist: (to Meredith) Does Andrew understand what is important to you and why you are upset?

Meredith: (crying, shakes her head)

Therapist: Can you try again to explain it to him?

Meredith: (crying) You don't know what it's like to be lied to. When I found those numbers, my world fell apart. You lied to me over and over. And now I don't know what was true and what was a lie. Was your trip to Philadelphia really business or was she with you? How will I ever know? It's my marriage, too. I have no control over my own life.

Andrew: (becomes pensive) I never saw it that way. I don't want you to feel like that.

Andrew reaches for Meredith's hand and the two sit together for a few minutes in a shared silence.

Even though Andrew was capable of soothing Meredith by taking charge and offering her reassurance, much of her crisis was based on Andrew's lying to her and her feeling of losing control over her life. It was not until Andrew could listen to Meredith long enough to join her experience that she felt genuinely responded to.

The therapist has identified some of the dynamics that likely contribute to the problems this couple is having, but more importantly, has created some new understanding that allows both partners to experience each other in a new way.

13 ―――――――――

Analysis of Projective Identifications

The marital therapist is a unique participant-observer to the ways each spouse perceives and reacts to the other. The events that are selectively attended to and the meaning that is attached provide a transparency to the inner object world of each spouse. Spouses are reactive to specific behaviors, attitudes, and responses in each other, and over time they define certain themes and issues as the basis for conflict. These repetitive cycles and the distortions that accompany them can be viewed as the nexus between past and present (Kernberg 1987a). The therapist's main task in marital treatment is to intervene in these spiraling destructive interactions and to redefine them so they can be approached in a more productive way. Proper analysis of the projective identifications can become the therapist's most potent tool for change.

In object relations family therapy, projective identification is considered an interactive dynamic, where family members are induced to take on and respond to projections from other family members (Zinner and Shapiro 1972). Scharff and Scharff (1991) suggest that if only the object representation is involved, then the activity is purely intrapsychic and should be considered a projection. If the external object contributes to the process, then the event has become interpersonal and can be considered a projective identification.

Projective identification is used here to describe a process wherein an unconscious conflict from the representational world is reenacted in the marital relationship. The nature of the conflict captures the meaning and affective experience that was internalized much earlier. Thus, the self is able to reexperience a traumatized self in relation to a punitive or neglecting object or to act like an internalized object against an undesired, expelled aspect of self. In both instances the partner is confused with the internalized representational world and is induced to take on the behavior and feelings that complement and complete the interaction (Siegel 1991).

Several analysts suggest that there is a reparative or adaptive aspect to the process of projective identification (Meissner 1978, 1982, Porder 1987, Tansey and Burke 1989). The externalization and reenactment of the past can be viewed as an attempt to find a different experience of the self in relation to the object. An attempt is made to turn a passive stance into an active one and to redo rather than merely repeat the conflict.

The theme that emerges must be thoughtfully explored, with opportunity for affective recall and experience. Spouses can then be helped to distinguish the internalized conflict from the present interaction. Projective identifications often illustrate frustrated expectations related to functions that had been relegated to the spouse. An individual who is dependent on a partner for esteem maintenance or reassurance will become enraged when the partner fails to provide the needed function. The rage can be regarded as an active attempt to demand from the new object those supplies that in childhood were needed but withheld. The past is re-created, and the new object is undifferentiated from intrapsychic representations.

Although individuals with primitive self structures are likely to experience and create especially intense projective identifications, the experience of projective identification does not seem limited to that population. Even adults who have achieved a strong sense of self and a healthy inner object world engage in interpersonal exchanges that are based on remnants of archaic representations. Psychopathology is evidenced in the failure to restore an observing ego and move beyond the rigid perceptions of self and spouse that service the regression. The healthy individual who has infused an interaction with unresolved conflict from the past is better able to correct overreactions when information that is contradictory to his or her perception and understanding is presented. An individual who has a less well developed observing ego is more prone to deny reality in order to preserve the reenactment of the past.

Projective identifications can range from slight distortions and overreactions to intense departures from reality. Because the process involves a repetition of interpersonal events that were previously experienced and internalized, the degree of denial and distortion is indicative of the extent of childhood trauma and the defenses that were active when earlier interactions were encoded.

The essence of a projective identification can only be fully appreciated by the therapist as the subjective reality of each spouse is completely untangled. The therapist must capture and relate to the affective experience of each spouse and the way each has constructed and assigned meaning to the interaction. Cues between the spouses may be subtle and not completely understood by the therapist, but the affective response in a projective identification sequence is swift and intense. Events and intentions are distorted in the decoding process as each spouse unconsciously blends current with past object representations. The interaction is perceived by the therapist as an emotional overreaction or an inappropriate response. One or both of the spouses experiences the interaction as a trauma and blames the other. Although the specific theme is rarely identical for each spouse, there must be complementarity or collusion for the interaction to escalate (Stewart et al. 1975).

The first task of the therapist is to focus the couple on the interaction and to clarify rather than contain the emotional experience until the subjective meaning to each spouse has been understood. Feldman (1982a) has stressed the importance of the cognitive distortions that accompany projective identifications. The therapist should not prematurely attempt to challenge these distortions but rather must pursue the meaning of the experience to each spouse.

The therapist can defuse a highly reactive emotional stance by validating and clarifying the feelings that each partner has experienced in the projective identification. Only after both spouses feel completely understood should the therapist attempt to engage their observing egos and help restore psychic equilibrium.

In helping the couple make sense of the interaction, it is useful to define the sequence as existing in the present but as echoing the past. A connection between how each spouse is made to feel and how they have felt in the past should be sought. When spouses are able to connect the pain they are experiencing with pain from the past, they are more likely to collaborate in resolving their dilemma.

Case Illustration

Carla and Pete (the couple discussed in Chapter 10) perceived each other as being totally self-centered and lacking in concern. Carla said she was tired of constantly having to please a partner who could never be happy and that the only way to ensure her own happiness was to focus on her own career and the things that she could do for herself. Pete felt totally misunderstood and neglected by Carla, and felt that she was only in the relationship for the things he could provide. He doubted that she truly cared for him or his concerns.

The preliminary history revealed that Pete was the eldest in a sibship of three sons. He had little recollection of his childhood, but initially described his family as a normal middle-class Irish-American family. He mentioned that his father had retired at a young age due to a deteriorating arthritic condition. Although Pete did not remember open conflict between his parents, there was a cold war that led to their separation when Pete was in college. His father committed suicide five years later.

Carla was reluctant to talk about her past. She was born in Austria and had two younger sisters. The children were physically abused by their father, who was a weekend binge alcoholic. Carla remembered her mother as a selfish, self-centered woman who did little to protect or nurture her children. Carla's grandmother was the only person who was loving toward her in her childhood, and she died shortly after Carla immigrated to the United States to attend college. Carla had married at a young age and divorced after her only child was born. She had married again for "mutual convenience" and divorced four years before she met Pete.

The couple had met in college. Each had pursued but not finished doctoral work and supported each other in their decisions to join the real world. Pete was attracted to Carla's good looks, confidence, and outgoing personality. Carla found Pete to be attentive, attractive, and accepting of her and her daughter. They were married within the year.

The couple had gradually found fault with each other's friends and soon were socially isolated. Lack of money created additional stress. Pete had changed careers twice, and Carla would only work in commission-based jobs. Although each superficially supported the other's career decisions, they also blamed each other for not being more successful. The couple rarely made love and avoided meaningful conversation, as it invariably led to conflict. When they fought, Carla would become intensely angry and threaten divorce. Pete would become cold and withdraw for days.

Therapist: I can see that your fights are devastating to both of you. Can you tell me about the last incident that led to a fight?

Carla: Pete is very selfish. We went out for dinner last Saturday and he knew I was wearing new shoes. Any other husband would have offered to drop me off in front of the restaurant and park the car himself. It didn't start the evening off very well, and we had a huge fight about it later that night.

Pete: I'm tired of hearing how selfish I am. Who woke who up in the morning? (to the therapist) I haven't been sleeping well and it's important to me to be able to catch up when I can. But Carla just had to play with the dog right in the bedroom, and bang all the dishes downstairs. (to Carla) Didn't you care that I was trying to sleep? How can you expect me to be in a great mood when you can't even show common courtesy to me!

Therapist: You know, both of you are feeling neglected right now. Not cared about and not important. Is that right? (Carla and Pete nod in agreement) Both of you have reason to feel that way. I have heard you talk about not feeling cared about before. Can we look at it together for a moment? You both seem to be saying that you have reached a point in your lives when it has become very important for your needs to be taken seriously and for you to be treated like you are valued. I don't think that the resentment and hurt you each experience when you talk about what happened on Saturday is new for either of you. I think it's more like a "bruise on a broken bone." It hurts a lot more if someone hits you just at the spot where you have a broken bone that has not completely healed. Pete, can you remember feeling not cared about like this before?

Pete: (in a perplexed way) I don't really remember my childhood very well. I don't think so.

Therapist: Can you remember times when your parents knew exactly what you needed and let you know how special and important you were to them?

Pete: No, not really. I don't remember too much.

Therapist: What about special events, like your birthday or Christmas? Did your parents seem to know exactly what you wanted?

Pete: I don't remember. I can't recall getting anything very special.

Therapist: What about feeling like if you needed something from your parents, they would do their best to get it for you?

Pete: I rather doubt that. That doesn't seem like my parents at all. I don't ever remember asking them for anything.

Therapist: You know, it's quite possible that you didn't ask them for special things, and perhaps that you didn't even expect special things from your parents. You strike me as being a very self-sufficient person. I wonder if that was something you learned when you were young. Can you think of any reasons that your parents might have needed you to be independent?

Pete: (very slowly and thoughtfully) You know, I never thought about it before, but my father developed severe arthritis when I was young. He had to quit his job it got so bad.

Therapist: The doctors couldn't help him?

Pete: No. He had it real bad. He used to be a draftsman, and his hands got so that he could hardly move them at all. His legs, too. He used to stay around the house. He was always in a bad mood, probably because it hurt so much.

Therapist: How did all of this affect your mother?

Pete: Well, she had to go to work to make ends meet. There were five of us, and she didn't have a lot of energy to be with us. You know, by the time she got home from work, cooked our dinner, did the wash . . .

Therapist: You seem to remember how tired your mother was.

Pete: Yeah. Tired and grumpy. But my brothers and I used to play on our own. I think my childhood was basically happy.

Therapist: Pete, I think you were a very sensitive, responsible son. I think you were very aware of your father's pain and your mother's exhaustion. They needed you to be invisible. How could you place demands upon a family that was already so overburdened?

Pete: (solemnly) I guess that's right.

Therapist: Pete, I'd like us to look at your feeling that Carla never seems to care about how you're doing. I think that you've reached a point in your life when you just won't be invisible anymore. You won't put up with it any longer. You want more from the people you love. I think that when you see Carla being very self-centered, you get very angry and frustrated. I don't think you want to minimize your own needs in order to take care of other people any more.

Pete: I think that's right.

Carla: I may have not been very sensitive when I woke Pete up, but he expects me to read his mind.

Therapist: You feel that Pete blames you for not knowing what he needs without telling you?

Carla: Absolutely! He never talks. I'm just supposed to know.

Therapist: I can tell that you don't like that very much. I wonder if that's a bruise on a broken bone for you? Can we look at it together?

Carla: (very stiffly) I prefer not to talk about my childhood. It's over and done with.

Therapist: There were painful things in your childhood that you would rather not remember?

Carla: Oh, I will always remember. But I can choose not to think about it and not let it matter any more.

Therapist: You would find it very hard to share some of these memories with me?

Carla: I can only tell you that my father used to drink. On the weekends mainly. But when he was drunk, he was a horrible person. He would strike me, my sisters, my mother . . . anyone who crossed his path.

Therapist: He would see you and then be angry.

Carla: He was drunk! There was always a reason. Some thing I had done wrong.

Therapist: This was very unfair. Why didn't your mother step in to protect you?

Carla: (indignantly) Huh! It was the opposite. My mother ran farther than anyone. It was up to everyone to take care of themselves.

Therapist: You spent a childhood being criticized and punished. I think that when Pete is angry at you unfairly, it makes you remember how unfair your father was. And when Pete withdraws from you for days, it must feel like when your mother left you to take care of yourself.

Carla: I should have learned back then never to trust or depend on anyone again.

Both Carla and Pete had survived childhood by learning not to trust too easily. As children, they had both compromised too much of themselves and had become overly self-sufficient and distrustful of intimacy. The projective identifications allowed them to protest their past in an active way and prevented them from getting too close to each other.

Carla's lack of attentiveness was a bruise that pressed upon Pete's broken bone of being forced into early self-sufficiency in childhood. Although Pete remained fairly cut off from his emotions, my interpretation helped him cognitively understand the intensity of his emotional reaction to Carla. By thinking about his past in relation to their current fight, he could begin to process the experience of being hurt and disappointed in the past as well as the present.

Pete and Carla each had been deprived of emotional confirmation and desperately needed to be noticed, validated, and responded to. Each had difficulty asking to be cared for but would be hurt and disappointed if the unarticulated need was not responded to. The cycle of hope, neglect, disappointment, and distance that had been established in their youths was repeated in their marriage, but this time both were more assertive and angry at their unresponsive object. As they began to realize the degree to which their current pain was related to unmet childhood needs, both became more able to talk about their feelings instead of jumping to the immediate conclusion that they were not cared about. Both enjoyed being able to make a difference to the other, and they found that when they were not criticized unfairly, they each had a great deal that they were prepared to give.

14 _____

Analysis of Countertransference

The therapist's awareness and use of self are important throughout the treatment process, but they can be especially useful in helping the therapist define and experience the dynamics that are most important to the couple. During the session, and occasionally outside of the session, the therapist experiences feelings and fantasies about him- or herself and the couple. The concept of countertransference explains these responses in a way that maximizes understanding of object relatedness.

Kernberg (1965) has distinguished the totalistic view of countertransference from the classical view. Instead of regarding the therapist's responses only as residues of personal conflicts that are irrelevant to the patient's therapy, the therapist's reactions are viewed as products of the patient's internalized representations that have been externalized or projected out. Because the therapist is induced to take on specific feelings and reactions, it is important that he or she is able to recognize and analyze the meaning of these subjective responses (Tansey and Burke 1989).

It is useful to compare the concepts of projective identification and countertransference. Many analysts have suggested that the two processes are the same and involve the selection of an external object upon whom aspects of the representational world are projected (Blum 1987, Joseph 1987). While the role of the therapist must be to hold and analyze the projected material rather than unconsciously accept the projection and engage in an irrational interaction, the reaction of the therapist is probably not different than those of other recipients (Meissner 1987). In both instances the client attempts to actively engage another person in the reenactment of an internalized conflict. Aspects of self or object representations are externalized, and the new object is provoked to accept and respond in a way that perpetuates the previously internalized conflict. It would seem that conflicts about the self that originated from an interpersonal context must be resolved in the interpersonal domain (Ogden 1987) and that intimacy and dependency reactivate these issues in therapy as well as the marital relationship.

The therapist who has limited self-awareness is easily swept up in the countertransference process and will act upon impulses in ways that are invariably counterproductive to the treatment. The therapist's resulting confusion, shame, and loss of control may create further resentment, which exacerbates and confounds the initial acting out.

The therapist who is able to appreciate countertransference as a transparency to the inner representational world of each spouse develops early awareness of the themes and dynamics that are most critical in the marital relationship. In many ways the therapist is a barometer; each change in the way he or she is feeling contains vital information that, if assessed and used properly, can enhance the marital treatment.

Case Illustration

Carly and Robert (the couple presented in Chapter 6) were very difficult to see conjointly because of the intense countertransference they stimulated in me. From the first session, I had found myself reacting strongly to each of them and to the dynamics they presented jointly as a couple.

Robert had threatened to end the year-old marriage, and Carly, in desperation, sought marital treatment. Robert presented as a casual, soft-spoken man in his mid-thirties. He was initially attentive to his wife and expressed discomfort about being seen by a therapist. Carly, ten years his junior, was quite reserved and seemed anxious to please her husband.

Therapist: Why don't you start by telling me what's going wrong for each of you?

Robert: I feel silly talking about it, but Carly is just irresponsible. She is incapable of running the house like a normal person.

Therapist: Can you be specific and give me some examples?

Robert: (getting increasingly angry) There are hundreds of examples. How many people leave moldy leftovers in the fridge all wrapped up in tinfoil so you can't even tell what they are? How many people have dead plants all over their house because they can't remember to water them? (Robert starts to shout) I don't do this to her. I work hard all day. All she has to do is manage the house!

As Robert grew increasingly angry, Carly stiffened in her chair and stared at the floor. I found myself feeling anxious about containing Robert's anger and also feeling uncomfortable as I evaluated my own housekeeping standards.

Therapist: I can tell you are very angry and disappointed. It sounds like Carly has really let you down, and you just don't know how things can ever change.

Robert: It's useless. I don't think she can change, and I don't think this therapy is going to help either.

Therapist: I think we have to slow down and try to understand your feelings. I can tell that you are very pessimistic and very upset. In order to really understand your situation, I need to talk to Carly, too. Let's see if we can hold off on making any decisions just now. (to Carly) What have things been like for you?

Carly: (in a soft voice with downcast eyes) Robert is right. I think this is all my fault.

Therapist: Can you tell me more about that?

Carly: I never meant to hurt him.

At this point, I felt strong compassion for Carly who seemed so helpless. I felt annoyed at Robert for being so harsh with her and protective toward Carly. At the same time, I was aware of feeling irritated at Carly for not being able to articulate her position and for not being able to stand up for herself.

Robert: That's it. This therapy is a waste of time. I've had it. It's time to go.

Therapist: Robert, just give me another minute to try to figure this out. I imagine you are both as uncomfortable as I am right now. Things get so intense so quickly between you. I feel like we've been through a storm together, but I can't tell which way the wind's blowing. Is either of you also feeling confused about what's going on here?

Robert: (as Carly nods in agreement) That's why there's no point to this.

Therapist: I understand why you don't want it to keep on going like this, and I don't think it has to. Let's try to calm things down together. When the two of you fight at home, it must get out of control very quickly, just like it did here. It is very important to your marriage to understand what goes on in situations like this. It would be hard to solve problems together if things get intense like this so quickly all the time.

Although I have been with many other clients who are angry, Robert flooded me with a sense of responsibility for his anger, as well as fear for its outcome. I was also provoked to feel inadequate and powerless. These themes were quickly revealed as being Carly's response to Robert as well. Given the intensity of my countertransference, I speculated that these themes would be important in Robert's childhood.

Subsequent history revealed that, as a child, Robert had been forced to be the emotional caretaker to a self-absorbed alcoholic mother and a vain, competitive father. Both of his parents considered themselves artists, and Robert's interest in "normal" activities, such as the Boy Scouts, was demeaned. Robert was constantly criticized and ridiculed by both parents and had acted out in self-destructive ways throughout his childhood and adolescence. Thus, the themes of destruction, critical self-evaluation, and responsibility were of the utmost importance, not only to Carly, but to Robert.

In a similar way, learning about Carly's childhood helped me make sense of my contradicting irritation and simultaneous need to protect her. Carly had been emotionally neglected by self-absorbed parents who were demanding and devaluing of her. Her attempts to protest led to further criticism, rejection, and abuse. Carly saw herself as defenseless and was numb to her feelings. Her only solution in relationships had been to merge with the powerful object. She had abused substances from an early age and could only express her anger through self-destruction and passive–aggressive defiance of expectations. Through her rapid merger, Carly created intense confusion and ambivalence in those around her.

These dynamics created the projective identification sequences that defined the problems in the couple's life together. Because she appeared inept, Robert would give her a list of chores that needed to be done to run the house. Carly would passively fail to meet his standards and would appear confused and defenseless. Later, when Robert felt bad that he had been so critical and angry, he would try to compensate and make it up to her. Robert would then feel overburdened and unappreciated, as he had in his childhood. Carly was frightened by Robert's anger, but also related to it as an expression of her own repressed feelings. Carly's fear of failing and her helpless dependence were similarly experienced vicariously by Robert. Carly's incompetence provided Robert with a sense of superiority, as he was able to devalue her in the way he had been devalued throughout his childhood. Robert's anger and potential loss of control were proof to both that self-assertion and independence would only lead to destruction and abandonment.

Because the projective identification was so intense in this couple, their emotional needs and reactions quickly spilled into the transference–countertransference. Robert and Carly were not able to soothe themselves, and they needed an external object to bring order to their lives. When they were unable to find that in each other, they demanded it from the therapist. Their panic around the destructiveness of Robert's anger was similarly displaced onto the therapist. If the therapist had been unable to contain and tolerate their anger and badness, the couple would have most likely projected their feelings of inadequacy and have quit treatment, believing that the therapist was not capable or good enough to help them.

15

Modifying the Splitting

Couples who fluctuate between extremes in the way they view
their relationship are usually able to acknowledge their tendency to split. It is essential for the therapist to identify and
begin to challenge this dynamic as early in the treatment as
possible. If the tendency to split is not identified as harmful to
the relationship and to each spouse's ability to maintain well-
being, the therapist will have problems intervening when it
becomes a destructive dynamic in the treatment. A spouse who
splits will quickly idealize the progress in therapy and develop
unrealistic hopes and expectations. Rather than learn to build
slowly, the unhealthy cycle of all-or-nothing will take over.
Now, the therapy as well as the spouse must be perfect, or both
will be vulnerable to rapid devaluation.

Attention to splitting can be especially important in the
beginning stages of treatment, when the couple is often most
pessimistic or desperate. The therapist who is able to help the
couple remember or get in touch with the more positive aspects

of their relationship can help them revive hope. By anticipating the tendency for couples to become overly optimistic and then bitterly disappointed, the therapist can forewarn the couple and help them observe and work with the dynamic, should it evolve.

As the therapist works to modify the splitting, the observing ego in both spouses must be strengthened. The goal is to help the couple find middle ground, and to find some way of soothing the intense feelings activated by the all bad self and object representations. When a spouse is intensely angry or upset, it is highly unlikely that he or she can recover sufficient observing ego at the moment to respond to cognitive interventions. In this instance, it is often sufficient for the therapist to acknowledge that it is difficult to see another point of view when intense emotions are present and to predict that the spouse will be able to see the other side when he or she feels calmer.

If the agitated spouse is able to accept the soothing functions of the therapist, it is often possible to reengage the observing ego and continue working with each partner's capacity to expand cognitive awareness and become better able to stay with the provocative material. Once the partners begin to accept their tendency to react to their relationship in all-or-nothing ways, they gradually become more comfortable in being able to predict the eventual resolution of the bad situation, which further facilitates their capacity to regain middle ground.

Case Illustration

Andrew and Meredith (the couple discussed in Chapter 12) both saw their relationship in all-or-nothing terms. Despite the fact that he had an affair, Andrew initially denied that there were any problems in the marital relationship for him. Meredith would similarly plunge into moments of despair, only to find her mood and outlook change rapidly if she was distracted by a friend or if Andrew was spending time with her.

Even within a session, Meredith's mood would change rapidly.

Meredith: We really don't have much of a marriage. You never talk to me about what's going on at work, and when you're at home, you just want to read or watch T.V. I don't think we have anything in common and I don't see why we should stay together.

Andrew: I never get the idea that you really want to hear about what's going on at work.

Meredith: That's not true.

Therapist: Andrew, when we met alone last week, you had a lot of things on your mind that were work-related. Would it be all right to share some of that with Meredith now, so I can see what happens when the two of you try to talk?

Andrew: It's hard to. . . . Well, lately I've been feeling confused. I worked so hard to get where I am, and now I don't know where I'm heading. There are so many young talented people coming up behind me, and the work sometimes doesn't feel as exciting or as important as it did a few years ago.

Meredith: What makes you think work needs to be exciting? Do you think that I go to work every day and say, "Today better be an exciting day for me"? You're spoiled. You asked for this responsibility and it's what you always said you wanted. You can't change your mind after all you've put your family through.

Therapist: Meredith, you have a lot of strong feelings. You strike me as being quite angry, and it sure makes it hard for Andrew to have the kind of conversation you say you want. What's going on?

Meredith: I am angry. For years I went through life as if I was a single mother. He was never there when there were problems with the kids. It was always work, work, work. Work came first. I came last. But it was what he needed to be happy. I've put up with too much for him to not be happy again.

Andrew: It's true that I worked hard, but you know that I wasn't just working for myself. Be honest. You liked it when I was promoted, when my paychecks got bigger, when people in the community knew who I was. You liked it a lot. And it's not true that I have never been there for the kids. Maybe I didn't take time off from work when they had the measles, but you know that we talked about the kids almost every night, and that I spend almost all my time on the weekends with the family. I haven't taken a vacation without you or the kids since we got married.

Meredith: (calming down) You're right. I guess I just get jealous that work means so much to you when I think that I don't matter at all.

Andrew: How can you say that after Friday night?

Meredith: (starts to giggle) Well, no one said we had problems in that department. We did have a good time, didn't we?

Therapist: Meredith, it's amazing to me how quickly you can go from being angry to being romantic and happy. Do you notice how quickly your moods can change and how your feelings about Andrew change from one minute to the next?

Meredith: I've always been like that. I guess I'm still an adolescent.

Therapist: I think it gets you into a lot of trouble and makes it hard for the two of you to solve problems.

Meredith: Why?

Therapist: When you're angry, things are so terrible for you that you really have a hard time emotionally. Your reaction is probably uncomfortable for you and definitely is for Andrew. I sense that you are so pessimistic that you don't have any confidence or hope that things will get better. But there's a reason behind those feelings, an important reason. When you change your mood so quickly, you also drop the problem that is causing your bad feelings, and it will never get resolved.

Meredith: Well, if I think about the problem again, my bad feelings will come back, so what's the point?

Therapist: We need to find the middle ground. The problem with Andrew can be very real, but it doesn't necessarily mean that he is all bad and the marriage is hopeless. It is possible to believe that Andrew is part bad and part good at the same time, and that by seeing both sides, you can have some anger, but also keep some hope.

Two sessions later Meredith announced that she wanted to quit couples' treatment.

Meredith: I almost canceled our session tonight. This is definitely it for me. I'm not coming back.

Therapist: What happened?

Meredith: It's the same story. We went out to a bar with some of Andrew's friends from work last Friday, and he flirted with all the women. He hardly paid any attention to me at all.

Therapist: That must have hurt a lot.

Meredith: And after we spent a whole session in here talking about my need for reassurance. What a bunch of baloney. I really thought that Andrew was going to change . . . that we were going to get close and things would get better.

Therapist: You and Andrew were feeling close after that session. You hoped that everything would get better all at once. When Andrew let you down, it felt like nothing had changed and nothing would ever get better.

Meredith: What's the use? I've had it with therapy!

Therapist: Meredith, remember a few weeks ago we talked about "all or nothing"? How sometimes you get so upset and pessimistic, and later everything seems fine again? I think that you're doing some of that right now. Things seem so hopeless to you that you can't believe they can be solved. I know you're feeling badly and disappointed. You think that the therapy is useless and I've failed you, like Andrew has. Do you think together we could work on what happened? Maybe we can find the other side. (to Andrew) What happened last Friday night? Were you aware of what was going on for Meredith?

Andrew: Absolutely not. She was at one end of the table and I was at the other. She was talking and laughing, and looking like she was having a fine time. I came over to her and sat beside her for a while. It's always like that when we go out together drinking. It's a crowd kind of thing. Meredith never once said she wanted me to stay with her more.

Meredith: Well, you were having a good time. I like to see you laugh and joke around. But I wasn't having such a good time.

Therapist: How did you try to let Andrew know that you needed something more from him?

Meredith: I guess I didn't. I just thought he should figure it out for himself.

Therapist: You want Andrew to change all at once and notice things so that you won't have to learn how to speak up for yourself and what you need.

Meredith: I have a hard time saying what I need.

Therapist: Let's take a closer look at that. But remember, by working together we can try to solve this. There's something here that we need to talk about and try to understand, but maybe things aren't as hopeless as you felt a few minutes ago.

Confronting the splitting helps the couple develop an observing ego and helps them stay with topics they would otherwise avoid or dismiss. If spouses are helped to observe their tendency to gloss over things when they are going well and give up in despair when they feel overwhelmed by the magnitude of a problem, they are better prepared to learn to work with the therapist in finding a middle ground. In the early stages of treatment, it is not likely that the dynamics that underlie and foster the splitting will all be resolved. However, if the therapist is able to provide structure and acceptance, the distress and rage that underlie the splitting will more likely be sufficiently soothed and contained to keep the couple engaged in the treatment process.

16 _____

Empathic Listening

A key component to a successful relationship is the capacity to understand and to feel understood. Without this foundation, it is difficult to negotiate productively or to make adjustments that are responsive to the situation at hand. Relationships must change in order to accommodate the normal developmental progressions and external stressors that all couples face. If spouses are unable to bring vital information about their needs and experiences into the marital system, there is no chance for the couple to work together or offer each other support.

Scharff and Scharff (1987) have defined the holding environment as a critical component to a successful relationship. The holding environment in a marriage encompasses mutual acceptance and responsiveness. Validation, which is a critical ingredient of intimacy, cannot be achieved without empathic listening.

Empathic listening requires each spouse to join his or her partner's experience. This cannot happen if a spouse feels attacked, blamed, anxious, or overly responsible, channeling all available energy into defending, avoiding, or redirecting the focus of the partner's input.

Marriage therapy presents an opportunity for spouses to develop the skills and self-awareness that will enable them to become more responsive to each other. Spouses that are least able to communicate empathically are often limited in their attempts by diffuse boundaries, excessive projective identifications, and/or unrealistic relationship expectations. These impairments in self and object representations quickly become revealed as the therapist works with each spouse to understand and correct distortions in the communication process.

Communication can be complicated at either the sending or receiving end. The spouse who is sending communication should be able to express his or her feelings and subjective experience in a way that is not attacking or provocative to the other. The information should be sufficiently focused so that the listener is not overloaded or confused. The sender must also be willing to articulate a position or need instead of expecting that the listener will implicitly know what he or she means or wants, like the omnipotent nurturing primary selfobject.

The empathic listener is simply invited to understand another person's experience. Often the listener is unable to engage in this process because he or she feels attacked, controlled, devalued, or overwhelmed. The therapist should help the listener untangle the reactions and projective identifications that have overtaken the capacity to simply relate. The concept of individuation is often an important component of communication problems; a partner who feels threatened when perceiving his or her partner as a separate person will have problems with the content and the act of independent communication of separate needs and feelings.

Some couples need help learning how to communicate feelings verbally instead of acting them out. The therapist can help them accomplish this by modeling responsive listening and by structuring the session so that the spouses are forced to talk together in new ways. This usually means interrupting sequences that begin to get out of control and working intensively with each spouse on the dynamic that has complicated his or her ability to communicate.

Case Illustration

Sam agreed to marital treatment after Riva threatened to take their two sons and return to Israel. The family had immigrated four years earlier and were in the process of becoming American citizens. Sam, age 39, had just completed his medical residency and was energetically invested in his career. Riva, age 29, worked part-time as a dental assistant and was also primarily responsible for raising their two school-age children.

In Israel, Sam and Riva had lived in close proximity to a network of family and friends. The couple had different interests, which they had been able to pursue with separate circles of friends. They also had a circle of supportive friends with whom they socialized as a couple. Although the couple had made some friends in the United States, their life-style was comparatively restricted, and aside from their work environments, they were almost totally dependent upon each other. Riva especially had become increasingly lonely over the years and complained that Sam never did anything she wanted him to. When she criticized or complained, Sam would withdraw for days, leaving her more lonely, needy, and depressed.

Therapist: Riva, as you talk to me about missing Israel, I see you trying to smile and put on a brave front, but I think you have some pretty intense feelings. What happens when you try to talk to Sam about how you are feeling?

Riva: Sam doesn't want to bother with me. He never wants to talk.

Therapist: I'd like to learn more about that. Can you try to talk to Sam here in my office?

Riva: (reluctantly, with downcast eyes) Well . . . you know how it is for me. It's not the same and I don't think I'm the same person I used to be. I'm just not happy. It's too lonely.

Sam: (joking) What, you lonely? With all your T.V. companions who make you laugh all afternoon? I'm telling Oprah what you said.

Riva: (starting to smile) It's different for you because you are so busy at the hospital.

Sam: (laughingly) So, now we should wish that I wasn't doing so well?

Therapist: Riva, you have a very charming husband who knows how to make you smile. But I want you to stay with what you were telling him about missing Israel. Talk to Sam again about feeling sad.

Riva: (reluctantly) It's true, Sam. I'm not happy and I think about Israel all the time.

Sam: (in a very abrupt, irritated voice) Either you deal with it or go back to Israel. You know where it is.

Riva: (totally silent with downcast eyes)

Therapist: Sam, I need to know more about what is making you so upset right now.

Sam: It's simple. I hate complainers. I am a doctor. If there is something wrong, then fix it; if it is minor, forget about it.

Therapist: When Riva talks to you about her feelings, do you feel the same as when a patient tells you about being sick?

Sam: Yes, but in this case I don't know what I am supposed to do. We both agreed that we could make a better life for ourselves here and everything is working out fine. I don't know what she wants from me.

Therapist: Sam, I think you're trying to do too much. Later I want to talk to you about taking responsibility for Riva, but for right now, it is important to just listen to your wife. I think Riva feels all alone, and if she can feel like you understand her, then you will have done something very special for her. No one is asking you to solve the problem for Riva. Do you think you could listen without feeling like you have to take full responsibility?

Sam: (raises his eyebrows and shrugs)

Therapist: (turning to Riva) Talk to Sam again.

Riva: Sam, I'm not unhappy all the time and I'm not blaming you. Sometimes I just start thinking how it would be for us if we were home and the children could just play outside and there would be so many friends and people for us to be with.

Sam: (quietly) I still feel like you are blaming me for taking you away from that.

Riva: No, but I miss it sometimes.

Sam: There is a lot to miss.

Therapist: (Riva has started to cry) Riva, I think it's okay to cry. Is there anything Sam can do? (Sam hands Riva a Kleenex, rubs her knee, and soothes her)

Empathic listening is often complicated by reactions that are directly related to projective identifications. Both partners have much to gain from the exploration and analysis of a projective identification. As each spouse is able to connect the events of childhood with his or her experience of the marital relationship, there is an appreciation of how and why the marital dynamics get so quickly out of control.

In many ways the reenactment of unresolved childhood conflicts in the marriage can be seen as a positive step in trying to make corrections and restore health. In order to turn a pathological interaction into a corrective process, each partner must take responsibility for trying to understand the internalized dynamics that are affecting the current interaction. Some spouses are more resistant than others to examining the beliefs and assumptions underlying the projective identification sequences. Clients who are not psychologically minded are often threatened by believing that there are dimensions of themselves that are not conscious or well understood. However, it is only through learning to observe their behavior and connect their feelings with their belief systems and past experiences that the most important hidden aspects can finally be confronted. Awareness is the first step toward change. The individual who is able to understand his or her experience in terms of the primitive self and object representations that have been revived is better able to reexamine needs, expectations, and his or her own behavior.

While it is the responsibility of each spouse to work through his or her own internalized conflicts, it is invaluable for the partner to understand the aspects of the interaction that he or she has assisted by taking on the required reciprocal role. Projective identification sequences rarely escalate without the full participation of both spouses. Insight and awareness can help the partner better grasp his or her own role in facilitating a destructive projective identification sequence and consider alternatives that will defuse or block the interaction.

Both Sam and Riva participated in the failure to communicate. Sam, for reasons unknown at the time, was agitated when his partner was needy or unhappy, and he felt overly responsible for causing and needing to solve emotional stress. Riva gave up too easily, and instead of defending herself and her right to be responded to, withdrew in a way that suggested she was bad or inadequate.

Therapist: Sam, you did a pretty good job of listening. I could tell that Riva's feelings make you uncomfortable. It's something I'd like to understand better. You seem to take on a lot of responsibility for other people. Are you the responsible one in your own family? Were you a pretty responsible kid?

Sam: (joking) Hell no. I was a total brat. I would say and do anything I wanted to do. All I had to be responsible for was getting good grades in school. The rest was simple . . . do what I want.

Therapist: Who was it the most important for that you got good grades?

Sam: My father. He wanted me to be a doctor since I can remember. Now this turns out to be a big mistake, because in Israel doctors are nobody . . . a dime a dozen. . . . Tennis players, that's another story.

Therapist: Sam, you want to make me laugh and talk about tennis.

Sam: (interrupting) Tennis is definitely worth talking about.

Therapist: I wonder, Sam, if you gave up a lot of things that you really wanted to do with your life in order to study hard and become a doctor. How do you think your life might have turned out if you had less pressure to be a doctor?

Sam: History. I'd be teaching history.

Therapist: Sounds like you knew that it was very important for you to come through for your father. That's a lot of responsibility for a kid.

Sam: My father is a good man. He did what he thought was best.

Therapist: You want me to think good things about your father. I wonder if we can both think good things about your father and still understand that he, whether he meant to or not, put a great deal of responsibility on his young son. What about your mother?

Sam: My mother never put any responsibility on me.

Riva: (laughing) This is totally true. She was incredible. He would come home from school and throw his books and clothes all over the house and she would pick up after him. She made him anything he wanted to eat. She still does. It makes my job impossible. Sam never knew how to boil water because of his mother.

Therapist: In families there are different kinds of responsibility. Who did your mother confide in?

Sam: (looking tense and somber) My father. My father adored my mother. He put her happiness above everything else. If my mother was upset or depressed, our whole house would shut down until my mother was feeling better. It was very clear. My mother was the most important person in my family.

Therapist: Were there many days when your mother was sad?

Sam: Well, she lost her whole family in Europe. Hitler and the war. . . . We didn't talk about it. She had been in a concentration camp herself.

Therapist: Sam, I think you have lived through a great deal of emotional turmoil in your childhood. In your family there were secrets about the past and fears about your mother's ability to cope. All of this would be passed on to a responsible, sensitive son. I think it makes you upset when Riva gets depressed because it was so difficult when your mother got depressed and the whole house was disrupted. I also think you might at some level be resentful of emotional women, especially when you think the reasons are trivial. Some of these things are very common in families of survivors, and we should talk about it more. (turning to Riva) It's not just Sam. We need to understand why you give up so quickly. Is this new for you, or was it like this when you were younger as well?

Riva: My family was very different from Sam's. Sam's father wanted Sam to be a doctor. My mother didn't care what happened to me. She never asked about homework. She preferred it when I skipped school. When I said I wanted to drop out when I was 16, she said that was a good idea. She never tried to encourage me or talk me out of it.

Therapist: Your mother liked it better when you were not succeeding in things that could take you away from her?

Riva: Yes. And also, my mother never did anything with her own life. All I remember is her lying on the sofa, watching T.V. If I had a problem, she didn't want to hear about it. But if she had a problem. Well, that was the end of the world.

Therapist: You learned not to have any needs, and not to expect anything from the people who say they love you.

Riva: (starting to cry) Yes. And now when I am in the apartment for too long, I think I am ending up just like her, on the couch watching T.V.

Therapist: It's important for you to believe that you are not like your mother. I wonder if it's hard for you to stay with your upset feelings because that, too, reminds you of your mother?

Riva: Yes, I never thought about it that way.

Therapist: Where does your father fit into all of this?

Riva: I'm not really sure. He was hardly there for us. I mean, he went to Brazil for months at a time. He had a business there. When he came home I know he loved me. But there were always fights between him and my mother. My mother was never happy with him. I think that's why he kept his business so far away. They really had a terrible marriage; I don't think there was a lot of time for me and my sister.

Therapist: Sam knows how to make you smile. I can see why you value that. Sometimes that must feel easier than fights.

Riva: (nodding) I had enough fights in my childhood.

Just as communication is a two-way process, the factors that complicate it are usually introduced by both of the partners. The challenge to the therapist is to keep both partners in mind and to unravel the distortions from both ends. This can be especially difficult when the couple presents the problem as being located in only one spouse, or when the therapist's countertransference causes an overidentification that leads the focus to rest on only one spouse.

It is as important to work with a spouse who gives up when his or her attempts to be understood fail as it is to work on the issues that complicate a partner's ability to respond. Both Riva and Sam were unable to talk effectively because of projective identifications that distorted their experiences of themselves and each other. Sam was threatened when Riva seemed like his distressed mother, propelling him back into the unhappy role he had assumed in his family of origin. Riva fought any likeness to her own mother and hated the part of herself that would complain or demand. She also repeated the experience of herself as being unimportant to her objects and used Sam's reactions to relive her feelings of being emotionally abandoned. In order to communicate effectively, each had to be freed from projective identifications that led each to be overreactive and unresponsive.

17 ═══════════════

Setting Limits on Destructive Behavior

Anxiety and rage cause spouses to say and do destructive things to each other. The therapist should intervene by setting limits on behavior that is out of control and/or damaging. This includes any act of violence or intimidation and reckless threats to divorce or to threaten the safety of the partner. The therapist should also limit the ways in which sensitive information that is learned in the therapy sessions is used at home. It is not uncommon for spouses to insult and ridicule each other in moments of anger, and the information gleaned in the marital sessions is often used as new ammunition.

Couples who cannot step back from destructive projective identifications or who are not able to adequately control their anger should probably not be seen conjointly. The excessive splitting, the lack of observing ego, and their poor impulse control indicate the need to strengthen individual boundaries and ego functions through individual sessions before meaningful and safe conjoint therapy can take place. However, the current marital situation and the dynamics that cause and exacerbate the projective identifications should be the focus of individual sessions with a reactive spouse.

Most couples respond well to limits that are set on acting-out behavior. This is especially so when the therapist is able to identify the interactive components and emotions that precede the destructive behavior. Spouses who can cognitively understand their experiences with anger and loss of control are better able to learn to take responsibility by removing themselves from situations before they get out of hand (Rosenbaum and O'Leary 1986).

Defining behavior that is destructive to the couple involves both subjective and objective criteria. Rage that does not culminate in violence or intimidation is difficult to assess, as individuals have different tolerance levels for anger. What is experienced as frightening to one spouse may be a normal and acceptable expression of feelings for the other. The range of acceptable behavior is also influenced by cultural norms and each spouse's experience with anger in the family of origin.

Physical violence should always be addressed as soon as the therapist learns about it. The abusing spouse may need to be referred to a special treatment group in order to learn to take full responsibility for the violence (Adams 1987). If the therapist avoids dealing with information that reveals physical violence, there is an implicit message sent that the couple is not doing anything wrong and/or the therapist is not capable of challenging the abusing partner. If the abused spouse does not experience the therapist as possessing sufficient power and strength to intervene in the violence, neither of the spouses will likely be able to engage in treatment in a meaningful way.

Substance abuse and alcoholism similarly need to be challenged by the therapist. The couple engages in and tolerates the abuse together, and they may both avoid or deny the importance of it to the relationship. The therapist who is told about drinking binges or drunken quarrels and fails to make explicit the role of the substance is joining the couple's denial (Davis 1981, Levinson and Ashenberg Straussner 1978). In this way, the therapist enables the perpetuation of a destructive dynamic and loses power and competency in the couple's eyes.

The therapist is often propelled into avoidance of these areas by countertransference related to fear of the couple's anger or rejection. The therapist's fear of having the couple prematurely terminate may be entirely correct, but it is also possible that the therapist will be able to work with these dynamics in such a way that both partners will accept the therapist's interventions.

Case Illustration

Tara and Paul had been married three years and had an infant and a toddler son. The couple was referred by their pediatrician after Tara complained about the couple's frequent and violent fights. Tara, who had been a model before the children were born, was impulsive and often distressed. She was very upset by Paul's lack of business success and complained about never having enough money. Paul worked in a commission-only sales job and was having a hard time staying committed to his work. He admitted that he was his own worst enemy and would lose jobs by failing to follow up or work cooperatively with customers he experienced as condescending.

In their second session the couple started to fight about Tara's pressure for the family to move to a larger house.

Paul: You know that we can only do it if I make that sale I told you about last week. If it falls through, then we hardly have enough money to pay the rent where we are now.

Tara: I'm sick of waiting. You're full of promises and no results.

Paul: What promises have I ever broken?

Tara: (in a disgusted tone) Oh forget it! You don't remember half of what you tell me. Why should I?

Therapist: I don't follow you, Tara. What are you talking about?

Tara: His promises. He's full of promises with a bottle of vodka.

Paul: You know I hardly ever drink.

Tara: That's what you wish. You were stoned out of your mind last Friday and Saturday, too, not to mention the pot you just bought.

Paul: That's not for me. That's for Fred's bachelor party, and you know it.

Tara: Yeah. And what else is for Fred's bachelor party? You go out all the time and I'm stuck at home with the kids. And it's no fun, Paul. I'm sick of it and I'm sick of that house, that dump!

Therapist: I think it's important to talk about the drinking and the pot more. Paul, it sounds like you might have a drinking problem. Can we talk about it together?

Paul: Me? I hardly ever drink. Now Tara . . . she's another story. Do you want me to tell you about the times I've come home and Tara's been hitting the vodka and she's passed out on the couch?

Therapist: What about that, Tara?

Tara: I don't drink any more now than I did before. Anyway, we didn't come here to talk about drinking. We need to talk about Paul's job and how there's never enough money. If he had more money, we wouldn't be fighting and we wouldn't be here now.

Therapist: I suspect it's all related. Your fights, Paul's behavior on the job, and the drinking. I'd like to know exactly how much each of you drinks so we can figure out whether or not the fights and the drinking are related, and whether there's more of a problem here than either of you thinks there is.

Paul: I really don't keep track of it.

Therapist: Would you be willing to keep a journal for me this week? Just jot down when and how much alcohol or pot you have each day. Are there other drugs involved for either you or Tara?

Tara: No, and I really think you're on the wrong track now, making such a big deal about the drinking.

Tara and Paul canceled their next two appointments. When I spoke to Paul on the telephone, he said he didn't think they would be able to come back and there was no point in booking more appointments.

Paul: It's not that you didn't help us. You really did. I did what you said about that diary, and you were right. I haven't had a drop for ten days and I know my drinking is related to how I feel about my job. But Tara has gotten worse. She's been drunk twice when I've come home. The kids weren't fed, they were crying. It was a real mess. And she's a wild woman when she drinks. She carries on about everything.

Therapist: I think that what you're telling me is very brave and a major step in turning your situation around. You know, Paul, I don't specialize in alcohol treatment, and even though you have stopped for ten days, it's another thing to stop forever. Do you go to A.A. or have any support with this?

Paul: No, and another thing, we really are strapped for money right now. It's the main reason we didn't come back. Tara is too proud to go to a clinic; she has to have the best of everything. But our insurance only covers a fraction of this counseling.

Therapist: Paul, I know exactly the place where you and Tara can get the help you need.

Paul: I don't think Tara will go.

Therapist: It would be a huge step if you went, even if Tara won't. They'll help you understand her drinking as well as your own, and I'm pretty convinced that once things start to change for you, Tara will agree to get help, too.

When I spoke to Paul two months later, he told me that he was successfully engaged in treatment and had stayed sober. Tara still refused to go, but since he was doing better at work, she was happier.

A year later, the referring pediatrician commented that the couple was doing great and that both of them went to A.A. He had not known that they ever had a drinking problem.

Throughout my session with Tara and Paul, I was faced with strong countertransference to stay away from the importance of alcohol. Tara related to Paul with scorn and contempt and threatened to treat me in the same way if I didn't accept her definition of the problem area and denial of substance abuse. Paul, in his own style of avoidance, found it easier to focus on his work inadequacies than the role of alcohol in his problems.

Although this couple terminated their treatment with me prematurely, they were only able to eventually get the therapy they needed by recognizing their need for help in controlling the substance abuse. The couple's impulsive, chaotic, and destructive interactions may not have been entirely based on alcohol, but without attempting to control that area of their life, all other attempts to engage an observing ego and get past the primitive defenses would likely have failed.

III

Practice:
The Middle Phase

18 _____

Stabilizing versus Insight-Oriented Treatment

Object relations marital therapy can be conducted on a brief or long-term basis. The more important issue concerns the goals of the therapist and the couple and whether there are expectations beyond stabilizing the relationship. These set goals and expectations determine the nature of the middle phase of treatment. As Slipp (1988) has pointed out, change in therapy can occur at the systemic, interpersonal, or intrapsychic level. It is possible to use an object relations perspective to achieve stabilization of the relationship with little intrapsychic change and minimal gains in each partner's understanding of his or her intimate self and its origin. In such instances, change will have occurred at the systemic and interpersonal levels.

Although treatment that focuses primarily on stabilizing the marital relationship is quite specific and focused, with some couples the treatment process can take several months or longer. Other couples, who have stronger representational resources to begin with, can accomplish successful marital stability in thirty sessions or less.

It is rarely clear to the therapist in the first session whether the couple has the capacity, interest, and motivation for insight-oriented work. With some couples, the existence of poor impulse control, rampant projective identifications, excessive splitting, and destructive acting-out behavior points to the need for immediate stabilizing treatment interventions. The presence of substance abuse, eating disorders, severe depression, or anxiety disorders would similarly preclude insight-oriented treatment as an initial goal. One of the most important indicators of the need to focus on stability versus insight is the strength of the observing ego. The couple's ability to observe, process, and reflect upon their own and each other's roles, needs, and feelings requires a cognitive and affective maturity that is prerequisite for insight-oriented work.

The distinction between stabilizing and insight-oriented work has contributed significantly to the treatment of individuals. Rockland (1989), Winston and colleagues (1986), and others have recently advocated a supportive approach to psychotherapy that is appropriate for work with individuals who have schizoid, borderline, and narcissistic intrapsychic structures. These individuals are not able to contain the anxiety that is raised in insight-oriented psychotherapy, and they do not possess sufficient ego strengths to endure the intense transference process that emerges in traditional analytic work.

In order to be effective with these populations, the therapist works from a more structured therapeutic framework, where an effort is made to clarify transference distortions in a reality-based way. The guiding treatment principle is to strengthen the patient's ego functions, which will translate into improved daily functioning and more successful interpersonal relationships. It is possible at any point to switch the focus of treatment to a more insight-oriented or traditional approach, but this should only be attempted after the ego functions are well intact. Most treatment involves some elements of both support and insight, but there are distinct differences in the goals and treatment interventions that belong to each approach.

These concepts can easily be applied to couples treatment, where the therapist is similarly confronted with a wide range of problems, expectations, and psychic resources in the couples who request treatment. The therapist who is only able to offer insight-oriented treatment indiscriminately will likely find that a high percentage of couples drop out of treatment prematurely or fail to make the kinds of gains the therapist had hoped for.

Because the therapist requires sufficient time to assess properly the couple's level of functioning, the engagement and early treatment process begins in much the same way for all couples. The therapist uses the early sessions to help the couple become comfortable with the treatment process and attempts to understand and work with the presenting problem in a way that helps the couple feel understood and hopeful of change. The spouses' commitment to each other and to the therapy are explored in order to uncover and work through resistances that might impede or prevent involvement or progress.

Projective identification sequences are defined and analyzed, splitting is confronted, and any acting out that is destructive to the couple's intimacy is discussed. The therapist helps the spouses examine the expectations they have set for each other and the ways they communicate and respond to each other.

Stabilizing treatment is designed to strengthen the spouses' ability to approach their interaction from a different perspective and to resolve their differences in a more productive and responsible way. Spouses learn to identify their own roles and issues in the recurring projective identification sequences and to block or step away from a sequence before it becomes fully escalated. If possible, the spouses learn how to get their needs met in ways that are complementary. Both spouses learn to use their observing egos to help modify distortions in their expectations and assumptions. As a result, the couple learns to relate in a more predictable way and to defuse interactions that formerly would have gotten out of control. Although the underlying needs may not have changed, the couple learns how to approach the situation more realistically and productively. Conflict that would formerly have festered and resurfaced can now be approached more directly, and both spouses consequently feel better understood. Stabilizing treatment is considered successful when the couple has restored or developed a better way of relating that can be sustained without the ongoing resources and interventions supplied by the therapist.

Insight-oriented treatment attempts to help each spouse better comprehend and accept those aspects of the representational world that may have been repressed or unconscious and have now surfaced in the couple's relationship. Projective identification sequences provide rich material to help the spouses discover and work through relationships with earlier objects and to explore aspects of the self that were previously dormant. Spouses are encouraged to participate in each other's therapy as they learn about the ways in which the past is re-created, as well as their specific roles in this process. As spouses learn more about their ways of relating, they are better able to respond differently to projections that may have previously induced unhealthy reciprocal responses. Spouses are also able to provide each other with support in the change and growth process.

19 _____

Long-Term Stabilizing Treatment

Couples who are deeply embedded in projective identifications and whose capacity for intimacy is restricted present a demanding challenge to the marital therapist. Because they tend to employ primitive defense mechanisms and because there are long-standing problems with boundaries and interpersonal expectations, the therapy is usually intense and compounded by countertransference strains. In addition, spouses often have simultaneous difficulties in other areas of their lives; because of the stress and defenses, they often have less energy available for the marital treatment.

Couples who have schizoid, borderline, or narcissistic object relations structures are difficult to engage in treatment. Issues of mistrust and control surface in the early sessions and must be dealt with. The couple approaches the therapist with unrealistic expectations, which provoke intense transference-countertransference. The therapist should focus on defusing and containing the intense feelings that the spouses stimulate in others and experience themselves. Efforts to create and sustain an observing ego occupy much of the treatment, as these couples tend to externalize their feelings and distort interactions. Although the therapist may spend considerable time examining and unraveling the projective identification sequences, understanding comes slowly, and the dynamics cannot always be defused or explained in a way that frees the spouses to interact differently. Splitting, projection, and blaming predominate in these couples, and their relationship is experienced in an intense and crisis-prone way. There is also considerable resistance to change, as spouses who have invested their partners with primitive self and object functions usually have difficulty relinquishing these ways of relating. Spouses who are arrested in the separation-individuation process become pathologically enlocked and are highly reactive to changes in their partners that they cannot control (Sharpe 1990, Singer-Magdoff 1990, Strothman 1985). The therapist must work slowly in order to reduce rather than stimulate anxiety.

Couples with impaired internalized object relations possess few successful ways of calming themselves or reducing anxiety. As a result, conflict quickly escalates, and spouses tend to act out or shut down in the face of uncontrolled rage and threats of abandonment. The therapist is often needed to provide soothing and structure, which help the couple face a stressful situation with strengthened resources. The couple may become dependent on the therapist to provide these resources and may triangle the therapist into their relationship in ways that revive primitive aspects of their representational worlds. Thus, the therapist must work to maintain neutrality and to avoid being overwhelmed by intense countertransference.

Case Illustration

Saul approached me after hearing a lecture I had presented on narcissistically vulnerable couples. He had been a clergyman who had trained in pastoral counseling, but had retired four years earlier because of a chronic health problem that had worsened. He and his wife of thirteen years had been in marital treatment earlier that year, but his wife Fran had abruptly terminated and refused to return. Saul was convinced that he and his wife were narcissistically vulnerable and could be helped if only she would agree to try therapy with me. Two months later he called to schedule their first appointment.

Saul was a tall, gangly man in his early fifties who was both demanding and simultaneously humble. He often avoided eye contact and spoke in an articulate but defeated manner. Fran was superficially friendly and cheerful, but was at the same time quite mistrustful and distancing. An attractive though slightly overweight woman, she was acutely reactive to her husband.

The couple had three children and agreed that they would have divorced years ago if it were not for the children. They lived in a small apartment and had a long-standing fight about the clutter that Saul created with his volumes of accumulated journals, computer material, and newspapers. Money was also a major conflict area, as Saul's disability check was the family's only source of income. Because the couple could not agree on a budget or method of paying bills, their financial situation was in constant chaos. The couple also had long-standing differences regarding the children's upbringing. These problem areas had worsened, and the marriage had deteriorated to the extent that Saul and Fran lived separate lives that were punctuated with abrupt and intense hostility. There was little conversation unless there was a problem with one of the children, and lovemaking was occasional and impersonal.

In their first session Saul alternated between humbly placating his wife and bitterly expressing his pessimism and disappointment. Fran responded to him as if he was a difficult or demanding child, and she seemed irritated by his dramatic gestures. Fran struck me as being resolved to an unpleasant situation. She enjoyed taking care of the children and interacted with her girlfriends when she was lonely. At night she read or watched T.V. to relax. By distancing herself from Saul, she could focus on the normal aspects of her life and block out the relevance of Saul's clutter and their lack of intimacy. Not surprisingly, the more she distanced herself, the worse the problems with the clutter became.

Engaging a Resistant Couple

I started work with this couple by sharing with Fran what I remembered from my initial conversation with Saul.

Therapist: Fran, I know that you and Saul were in therapy last year but that things didn't work out well for you. I wonder what has happened to make you agree to try again. I am also curious if there are leftover feelings from that experience and how we can try to make this therapy worthwhile.

Fran: (in a polite but condescending and distancing way) Frankly, I don't really believe much in this "talk" therapy. I'm only here because Saul insists on it, and I haven't the faintest idea what you could do to make this worthwhile for me.

Therapist: When I was setting this appointment up with Saul, I had to give him three or four alternative times. I know you have three young children and that you do not have a lot of free time on your hands. What did it take for you to agree to try therapy again?

Fran: (laughingly and again with a slightly condescending voice) If you must know, Saul and I have made a deal . . . in writing. I come to these sessions, and Saul will look for a larger apartment.

Therapist: Okay. You come here for Saul, and Saul gives you what is important to you. Can you tell me a little about why the new apartment is important to you?

Fran: You have absolutely no idea what my life is like. It would take hours and hours to fill you in.

Therapist: That's the hardest part of starting over with a new therapist.

Fran: I've been in this situation before, talking and talking, and nothing happens.

Therapist: How can this be different for you so that the things that you want the most can change?

Fran: (with a sarcastic tone) Look, you seem like a very nice lady, but this is a very complicated situation. I have agreed to come, and I will for at least ten weeks. But I intend to take things with a "just wait and see" outlook.

Therapist: You seem to be saying that you don't want to expect too much. Expecting too much and being disappointed might turn out to be an important theme in your relationship. (tears welled up in Fran's eyes)

Fran's initial resistance and devaluing of me were clear indicators to proceed slowly and avoid a control struggle. Because of this, I suggested to Fran that it would take a little time for us to get to know each other and that we could talk about therapy and her expectations after she had a chance to know me better and see how I worked. I respected Fran's need to establish a distance from me. I was also painfully aware of her anger, although unclear whether it was meant for Saul, who had been a therapist, her former marital therapist, or me.

Therapist: (to Saul) I wonder if you also have thoughts about starting with a new therapist.

Saul: (with a collapsed posture and expression of deep suffering) This relationship is extremely complicated. I have to provide you with a great deal of information in order for you to understand our predicament and be able to help us.

As Saul started to present his history, I found myself struggling with a nurturing response to his pain and simultaneous irritation at his self-pity and need to control. I interrupted Saul to comment that he had rushed by my initial question and seemed intent upon making up for lost time. Saul seemed delighted by my confrontation, and although he was defensive about his intent, he became more alert and dynamic.

Therapist: (to Saul) Why don't you tell me about being a therapist who probably had ideas about how treatment should begin.

Saul: I never worked with couples, but I have a pretty good idea of what's wrong with Fran. Fran's father died when she was an infant and there were no men in her family.

Therapist: (interrupting) Saul, I'm more interested in your talking about yourself right now. What ideas do you have about starting therapy over again now?

Saul: (in a sad and pensive voice) I have been in analysis twice and neither was successful. Do you know. . . . ? (naming a nationally renowned analyst)

I began to sense a pride that was attached to Saul's evaluation of being "complex" and his underlying defiance against being helped.

The early sessions with Saul and Fran focused on engaging the couple in treatment. Fran had become totally detached from the relationship and avoided facing Saul and all of the unpleasant qualities that he brought into her life. As I pushed her to tell me about day-to-day life at home, her indifference and *laissez-faire* attitude crumbled, and she turned on me with rage. Fran told me that I was a fool to believe anyone could change anything in Saul and that she was furious at me for trying to make her try again. I accepted Fran's anger and experienced with her the helplessness and futility of the therapy. I also sensed the depression and fragility that underlay the rage.

I provided a holding environment for Fran's despair and then told her that I was in a quandary and needed her guidance.

Therapist: Fran, even though I have not known you very long, I am impressed with your resourcefulness and competency. It is important to me that you have decided that it is useless to try again. At the same time, I can see that you've already put a lot of energy over the years into trying to change Saul and improve your life. I don't want to underestimate all of the work you have done, but there is a part of me that perhaps, in a naive way, believes there are still things that we could do to make it different this time for you.

My efforts to acknowledge Fran's resistance and to give her control over the pace provided her with the element she needed to feel safe. At home she had no control and had to withdraw; here she was supported and could become engaged. I had not fully censored my response, and the use of introducing my naivete was largely counter-transference. To my delight, both Fran and Saul picked up on this theme. In a marital system that had lost hope, I was endowed with their own split-off hopes and naive wishes that their marriage could improve.

Fran: (thoughtfully, and in a more receptive way) Each time I have tried to make this relationship better, I have been totally crushed by Saul. I do not believe that Saul is purposefully trying to destroy me, and I have finally accepted that Saul has no control over his moods and his need to clutter. You see, if I think of Saul as someone who is just sick and not doing this on purpose, then he is not responsible for all the pain I have gone through. If I have no expectations for Saul, I cannot be hurt by him. I feel sorry for him, but I don't think that he can change.

I restated what Fran had told me and then commented that she seemed to be talking about an important theme that many couples struggle with. I suggested to Fran that she was talking about being dependent on another person for her happiness versus being totally self-sufficient and more in control. I added that while all spouses had to find a balance with this theme, there were things that went on between her and Saul that made it difficult for each of them. By normalizing the struggle and defining it as a theme that they both struggled with, I tried to diminish her feelings of failure and engage her observing ego in looking at her relationship in a new way. At this point in the process, I did not explore or confront unrealistic expectations or the distortions, in her subjective experience, of Saul crushing her.

Saul became quite responsive and began to tell me about Fran's reasons for being self-sufficient.

Saul: (in an animated way) Fran does not know how to depend on another person. Her father died when she was an infant and her mother left her to return to work when. . . .

Fran: (interrupting in an agitated manner) You are not my therapist! Stop trying to be the expert of what's wrong with me and stop blaming me for what's wrong with this marriage.

Saul looked to me to join his frustration in working with an irrational wife.

Therapist: (to Saul) You seem to be appealing to me for something right now. Do you want me to think that Fran is out of line?

Fran: That's what he does in therapy — it's him and the therapist against me.

Fran and Saul erupted into a series of accusations and counter-accusations. I interrupted the sequence that had started between Fran and Saul and attempted to restore calm. I suggested that they needed to work with me in a more predictable way.

Therapist: It is clear to me that you both have strong feelings. I want there to be enough room in each session to really understand exactly what each of you is feeling. I need each of you to allow the other to answer me without interrupting. I promise you both that there will be enough time for you to respond to your partner and to have the floor. Let's try to calm down a little. There are a lot of feelings and frustrations that have built up over time, and each one is important. If we flood the room with everything that's wrong at one time, it will be overwhelming and impossible to solve.

Throughout my work with this couple, my own urge to respond to several things at one time had to be constantly checked. In this marital system, the flooding provided a distraction and led to the chaos and related anxiety that prevented Fran and Saul from using their observing egos. Structure and soothing became critical to the process of engaging both in the treatment.

Linking Past and Present

Saul had his own way of avoiding treatment and engaging with me in a meaningful therapeutic alliance. Saul tried to occupy the sessions with history and psychological explanations that helped him avoid his own feelings and blame Fran. He reacted strongly against my support of Fran and began to engage in a power struggle with me, using his need to tell the complete history as a way of maintaining control. If I tried to push Saul to observe himself or respond to a feeling, he would use his failed attempts at analysis as a reminder that greater experts than I had failed.

In one session, after Saul had done this twice, I decided to confront the issue.

Therapist: Saul, it is important that you want to tell me about failing in analysis. You are an interesting and complicated man. On one hand you seem to be defeated, but at the same time you are showing me what a fighter you really are. Every time I want you to talk about feelings, you prove to me that I cannot really help you in that way. So we have a dilemma. I want to support the part of you that is strong, but the part of you that is the fighter is the part that won't let anyone help you change. I think when you stand up against me, you are unusually strong, but it ends up pushing me away. Are there ways that you are able to feel strong and powerful and let other people get close to you? (Saul surprised me by looking totally defeated and self-pitying)

Saul: (with downcast eyes) I don't think that since my mother died I've been able to do that.

Therapist: I would like to know about your mother and what it was like for you when you were little.

Saul: My father never loved me and never tried to make me feel good enough about myself. The only person who had ever loved me was my mother.

Saul shared his childhood memories for several minutes, recalling his mother's interest and support. His mother, confined to bed with a heart ailment, waited eagerly for Saul's daily arrival from school. In many ways he was her contact with the outside world, and she was deeply invested in his growth and success.

After Saul finished talking about his close and loving relationship with his mother, he added that he married Fran because he
thought she could make him believe in himself again, but she turned
against him. He thought he was marrying his mother, but he got
another father instead.

It became clear to me that Saul had an impoverished representational world. He was completely reliant on external resources to
sustain his self-esteem, and he expected Fran to be totally responsible
for replenishing his good feelings. At the same time, he resented her
strength and independence, and experienced her as being as rejecting
and unresponsive as his father had been. By standing up to Fran
through passive opposition, Saul was repeating his childhood relationships with both his father and sister.

I commented on Saul's loss and said that it was important that
without another person valuing him, he didn't know how to feel
worthwhile and important. I suggested that a man who was also in
early retirement probably had extra burdens placed on him in finding
ways to feel competent. His health problems and related exhaustion
undoubtedly exacerbated his ability to feel good about himself and
added to problems of not feeling loved that had existed from his
childhood. When Saul believed that I could accept him without being
critical or demanding, his defenses softened and he was able to
generate sufficient trust in me to engage in the treatment process.

The Middle Phase of Treatment

Once the couple had engaged in treatment, there was a dramatic
change in the nature of the sessions. The couple would use up all of the
time and had difficulty ending a session and leaving. Neither Fran nor
Saul was ready for self-examination in an insightful way, but they
brought disturbed feelings into the sessions, looking for soothing and
structure. They had little recall of the work that was done in previous
sessions and, unlike couples that have stronger resources, they were
not able to talk together about their treatment outside of the treatment hour.

As Fran began to involve herself in the relationship again, there
was intense conflict at home that led to screaming matches and

withdrawal. This led to work in the sessions on splitting and limit-setting. Treatment also included examination of the expression of anger and other feelings.

Therapist: There seems to be a lot of tension in the air today. Is anything going on between you two?

Saul: This has been a terrible week. Horrible beyond words. I am ashamed and disgusted to tell you what goes on in our house.

Therapist: I can see you are both upset. Can you tell me what happened?

Saul: It's not even important to talk about why we fought. Only that it got out of control.

Fran: (agitated, interrupting) Oh, yes, it is important to talk about why we fight. I am still angry.

Therapist: Perhaps you would like to go first, Fran.

Fran: It's not easy managing three children, and I don't need four. I don't mind cooking special meals for Saul. He has health problems and I don't mind. And the children won't eat the same things, so I end up cooking for them, too. Sometimes I think that that's all I do. But I cannot take care of Saul all day.

Between the two interrupting each other to add information, I finally pieced together that Fran had been in the kitchen cleaning up the children's lunch dishes while Saul and the toddler were finishing their lunch in the dining room. The toddler wanted to sit on Saul's lap, but Saul had not finished eating. With the toddler on his lap, he called to Fran to take the baby. Fran resented the interruption, cleared all the remaining lunch dishes from the table, and told Saul he needed to be more firm with the baby. Saul had not finished eating, and the two started to fight over his plate. This led to a food fight in the kitchen, and eventually to Fran's ripping Saul's shirt.

Therapist: If I understand it right, Fran, you felt angry and resentful that Saul could not do a simple task when you felt so stressed by all the work you still had in front of you. Saul, you felt completely unsupported by Fran, and then punished by her when she took your food away without letting you finish.

Saul: Yes, like a bad child.

Fran: He's a grown man. Why can't he act like one?

Therapist: There was clearly a lot of tension and anger building up. I think this fight was over more than clearing the table. Each of you reacted very intensely, and I think that there were hot spots being touched for both of you. Before we try to understand these, can I ask a little more about your relationship with the baby, Saul? (Saul nods approval)

Therapist: You seem to have a hard time saying no to little Matthew. I think you didn't really want Matthew on your lap, but didn't know how to say no to him.

Saul: I don't think that children should be overly frustrated before the age of 4.

Therapist: You think that you react to Matthew in this way because you're concerned about his psychological development?

Saul: Definitely.

Therapist: Saul, I think you have a hard time saying no to Matthew because you don't like what happens when he's frustrated.

Saul: You mean because he cries?

Therapist: Yes, and because he doesn't act like he loves you when he is angry at you, and I think you need to believe that Matthew always loves you very much.

Saul: (after a silence) That might be true. He's the only one who really loves me. Fran has taken over the other children, I can see it happening. But Matthew is still mine.

Fran: (interrupting) Oh, Saul, don't be silly. How can you mean that I've taken over the other children? They both love you. And

Matthew loves me, too. How can you think about dividing the children like that?

Saul: You're blind.

Therapist: I get the sense, Saul, that you blame Fran for what's going on with the children.

Saul: I do. The older children don't respect me. They don't come to me for decisions, just their mother.

Therapist: You feel that the children don't treat you like a father in the way that you want to be their father.

Saul: Exactly. I want my opinion to matter more.

Therapist: Saul, I wonder if these two areas are related. On one hand, you love your children very much and don't want them to be angry with you. When there is a limit that has to be set, you call in Fran, kind of establishing in everyone's mind that Fran is the boss, the one who has to be listened to. But later, when the children have a problem, they go to Fran instead of you, and you get very hurt because you're ready to help them, but they don't seem to think of you as the kind of guy who can be in charge.

Saul: Fran should send them back to me. She should make them go to me when they need to talk.

Therapist: Saul, you're depending on Fran again to take charge. What could you do to feel in charge and make all the children know that you are a parent who is strong enough to take their problems to?

Saul: You are trying to make me discipline the children and I can't do it.

Therapist: I think if we can separate the ideas of love and discipline, things will be much easier for you. Let's look at how things happened in your home with your parents.

Saul: My mother never needed to discipline me. I adored her. If I ever thought I had let her down, I would be crushed. I would have done anything for her. I did do everything for her.

Therapist: And your father?

Saul: I told you about him. He was cruel and sadistic. I never did anything that was good enough for him. Not once. Not my grades, not the speech contest I won, nothing. But he was the first person to criticize me . . . yell at me for what I didn't do. Always complaining about me. He never gave me anything.

Therapist: (gently) Saul, is it really so surprising that inside you want to feel like your mother toward your own children . . . to be the parent who is always kind and loving, the parent who is never critical and punishing? I think you feel too much like your father when you have to discipline the children. And you are afraid they will hate you, like you hate your own father.

Saul: (pauses) Well, . . . maybe. . . . I don't want my children to think about me in a bad way.

Fran: And if the children get too close to me, then Saul feels left out.

Therapist: Yes, left out like he was between his sister and his father. And if the children see you as the good parent, then they must see him as the bad parent, because in Saul's mind, you're one way or the other. There's nothing in the middle. Can we look at what happened from another angle? I think it is important how Fran gets worked up to criticize and punish Saul.

Fran: What do you mean?

Therapist: Saul, Matthew needed to be told to stay in his high chair and finish his lunch, and I think you knew it. When you gave in and put him on your lap, I think you were upset with yourself. By calling Fran into the picture, she could take over for you and be the one to say what a failure you were.

Fran: What was I supposed to say? How great he was doing?

Therapist: I don't know, Fran, but I do know that as long as Saul sees you as a demanding and rejecting "dragon," he can concentrate on feeling sorry for himself. In truth, I think the demanding, rejecting "dragon" lives inside of Saul and that you can only tame a dragon where it lives.

Fran became irritated and angry at this interpretation. She confronted me with her right to be angry at Saul. As Fran began to talk about not putting up with his craziness anymore, I held her feelings. I suggested that standing up for her own rights was something new to her and something that we needed to look at together. Fran was able to talk about her painful childhood of being raised by an aunt who disliked her and made it clear that she was only there because of Fran's mother's desperate situation. Fran had never been responded to by her aunt or mother and had learned to accept her lack of importance. In her family, Fran's needs were less important than everyone else's. Fran's earlier position of seeing Saul as a sick person enabled her to perpetuate self-sacrifice and the belief system that her needs were less important. Now Fran had to begin to struggle with her own rights to be heard and responded to and her fury and rage for having come second all her life. Fran's anger was now directed entirely at Saul, who had deep-seated fears of anger stemming from his own childhood.

Therapy continued to provide a holding environment, where each could be listened to and be validated. Each spouse was so needy and reactive that my early attempts to develop empathic listening skills for them to use with each other failed. Fran and Saul also began to compartmentalize treatment as a separate aspect of their lives and were unwilling or unable to work at home on any of the issues raised in session. I increased the number of sessions to twice weekly in order to help maintain stability and deescalate the projective identification sequences that exacerbated the conflict at home.

In each session a new crisis or conflict emerged. Some of the conflicts arose around money, some over Saul's clutter, and some over disciplining the children.

Work with these problems provided access to Saul's tendency to split and his unrealistic expectations of Fran. Saul's style of depending on Fran to accomplish things for him and his rage when she failed him were the subjects of many sessions. Saul's depressions, which exacerbated his exhaustion, pessimism, and self-pity, were also attached to this dynamic. As Saul began to take small steps to act for himself in setting limits on the children and getting his own needs met, his depression started to lift. Saul assumed responsibility for putting the children to bed each night, which involved setting limits regarding turning off the lights. He also began to take responsibility for dealing with tradespeople whom he had formerly avoided. In the past he had pleaded with Fran to deal with a tailor who had not fixed a pair of pants to his satisfaction. With my support, he confronted the tailor himself and avoided the former cycle of depending on his wife and displacing onto her the anger he felt toward other people.

As Saul became more autonomous, Fran became more interested in him and aware of her own ambivalence about his separateness. Fran began to express her own needs to be treated like a woman, and she became more aware of her needs to be valued and made love to.

Work was also done with Fran around her own tendency to split. Fran saw the world through rosy glasses and defended herself from pain by dismissing the bad and concentrating on the good. She saw Saul's small steps as a promise of drastic, immediate change, and when he disappointed her for the first time, she became extremely pessimistic. Fran was helped to remember her childhood and the expectations that had been placed on her to be perfect in order not to be a burden. Fran slowly began to realize that small setbacks did not mean a disaster, and she became more tolerant of failure in herself as well as Saul.

For the first time in years, Fran and Saul started to enjoy the time they spent together. The couple went out for dinner and started to demonstrate affection toward each other. Each was becoming more aware of the other as a separate person with individual strengths and needs.

In working with this couple, there were numerous setbacks and reversals. After one particularly bad week, Fran reverted to her splitting and pessimism that nothing was really ever going to change. She was irritated at her need to depend on me to solve her marital problems, and frustrated with how much energy she had put into the therapy. Fran said she wanted time away from treatment. Between the time that Fran announced this at the end of one session, and the following session, the decision to end treatment became a major control struggle between Saul and Fran. Saul was convinced Fran would never return, that she would revert to her old ways of being self-sufficient, and would completely shut him out of her life again. This struggle mirrored other attempts for Fran and Saul to get their needs met at the same time and the difficulty they had negotiating differences on a day-to-day basis. Fran perceived Saul as stubborn and unresponsive, and his problem with clutter was getting worse. Therapy remained the only weapon she felt she possessed.

My decision was to validate how their different perspectives could allow them to add to each other's lives. I commented that at the moment both had a need to accomplish something that they saw as being productive and necessary. I saw Fran's need to withdraw from therapy as a personal test on becoming dependent and facing disappointments versus being totally self-sufficient. I said I would respect Fran's right to work this out in the way she needed to, and I asked her to make at least one appointment with me within six weeks to let me know her progress in resolving this issue. I explored with Saul his reaction to having the treatment interrupted, and I validated his pessimism and anger. I suggested that his irritation was being stimulated by Fran so that he could feel as out of control about what was important to him as she did about what was important to her. I thought it would be valuable to find out what Fran's commitment to change was and said that I was much more optimistic than he.

Four weeks later Fran called to resume treatment. She felt revived by the break and had renewed energy to commit to the relationship. For once her needs had come first, and she had been respected and permitted to act for herself. Saul had done some thinking about helplessness and was beginning to see how his clutter provoked Fran to express feelings that he also had.

Work with this couple continued to emphasize stability rather than insight. Both were helped to understand their reactions to each other from an interactive perspective so that they could prevent projective identification cycles from being destructive. The couple was slowly helped to challenge their expectations of each other that were unrealistic and to identify the importance of the recurring themes in their interaction. Their tendency to split and their reactions to the marriage when it was perceived as "all bad" were worked with to prevent the cycles of passive-aggressive anger and withdrawal.

After two-and-a-half years of treatment, the couple was able to make a joint decision to move to another state, where they could afford larger living accommodations and a more relaxed life-style. The move involved numerous decisions, and great strides were made in listening and responding to each other without feeling controlled or demeaned. The couple still tended to be overly reactive, but they were able to take more responsibility for checking out each other's intentions instead of jumping to conclusions that perpetuated the projective identifications. Fighting was diminished, and there were even occasional times when each could compliment the other on bringing something different and valuable into their shared life.

20 _____

Short-Term Stabilizing Treatment

The marital therapist is often confronted by couples who seem to possess the capability for insight-oriented work but who, for the moment, are experiencing a crisis and are only interested in recovering their precrisis way of relating. As Rockland (1989) has pointed out, motivation for insight is always a precondition to be considered in whether to provide supportive versus traditional psychotherapy with individuals. In the same way, the couple who wish only to return to the level of intimacy they previously knew will likely be resistant to long-term work. It is possible to help the couple recover stability, acquire a minimal degree of insight and self-awareness, and terminate treatment even though there are issues that have not been worked through and are likely to resurface in the future.

It is always important for the couple and the therapist to be working together on shared treatment goals. If the therapist becomes disappointed in the couple's lack of interest in insight-oriented work, the countertransference will contaminate the therapeutic alliance. It is wiser to provide the level of intervention the couple is able to commit to and leave the door open for the couple to resume treatment at a later point in their lives.

The decision of when to confront and attempt to work through resistance versus when to allow resistance to dictate the termination process is complicated. Some of the issues to be considered include values, resources such as time and money, and the couple's right to self-determination. The therapist cannot ignore the defenses and underlying intrapsychic factors that cause the couple to be anxious about confronting unknown areas of themselves or fears they may have about becoming dependent on the therapist. At the same time, the therapist should be aware of differences in the value the couple place on insight and the level of intimacy they seek. If the therapist is able to articulate these concerns and work with the couple's observing ego and the therapeutic alliance, there is a good chance that the differences between the therapist and the couple can be understood, respected, and worked with in a way that in the long run will benefit the couple.

Case Illustration

Sarah and Roger had been married for two years and had developed a high level of mutual dependency. A crisis developed when Sarah began to pressure Roger to have children. After feeling confused and depressed for several weeks, Roger told Sarah that he didn't believe their relationship was secure enough to bring children into their lives. He thought that the only solution was divorce. Sarah was shocked and upset by this, and she initiated the couple's treatment.

Roger was the second of five children, but was the favorite child of his mother. He described his mother as a competitive, intelligent woman who was highly perceptive and successful. In contrast, he described his father as a reclusive man who spent most of his free time gardening. Roger's parents had not been close to each other, and they slept in separate bedrooms.

Sarah was an only child and had been abandoned by her father when her parents divorced when Sarah was 6 years old. She had developed an intense but ambivalent relationship with her mother, who relied heavily on her daughter to meet all her emotional needs. Sarah had become her mother's confidante and extension, going to the college her mother selected and dating the men that her mother thought best for her.

Despite the stress they were under, the couple seemed attentive and responsive to each other. Sarah felt they had a perfect marriage and couldn't believe that Roger was unhappy with their relationship. Roger's only concrete complaint was that Sarah was too moody. Roger needed to be perfect at everything he attempted, and when Sarah was irritated or depressed, he felt responsible for reversing her unhappiness.

The early sessions revealed that the couple was uncomfortable with needing help and exposing their problems to a therapist.

Roger: I don't mind telling you about my family, but I don't see what it has to do with my marriage right now.

Therapist: I sense that you are a private man, and it is difficult for you to be in this position.

Roger: I am here because I am trying to save my marriage and you're the expert. But I don't see how this information will help me.

Therapist: I ask questions about your family because I believe that much of what you learned about being a husband to Sarah came from what you observed and experienced in your childhood. I think the relationships you had with both of your parents come into play here. But I also think that these are sensitive areas for you, and perhaps talking about them makes you feel uncomfortable.

Roger: There is no reason for me to be uncomfortable . . . but perhaps I am. I think this is just a new situation for me and I'm usually the one who is in control.

Therapist: I think it's important for you to be able to feel like you have control over what is happening here. When I probe too deeply, it's not really helping the situation, and I don't know you well enough yet to know when you are uncomfortable. Could you find a way to let me know when that is happening? You should have control over things like that, and you should also be able to ask at any point what the purpose or direction of our conversation is.

Sarah and Roger agreed to postpone a discussion of their different viewpoints on starting a family and concentrate on how they affected each other in other aspects of their relationship. Both Sarah and Roger had grown up in families where there was tremendous pressure on them to excel. They were very competitive in every sphere of their lives and held high expectations for each other. Because they each needed to see their relationship as perfect, they avoided certain areas of conflict. If they were disappointed or frustrated with each other, they tended to communicate their expectations as clearly as possible, with the expectation that their partner would automatically comprehend and change.

If the problem could not be solved in that manner, they both tended to dismiss its importance. At the same time, they each would withdraw in a way the partner chose not to confront or deal with. As a result, the couple rarely made love because of Sarah's moods, and their time alone together was limited because of Roger's active social calendar. Occasionally Sarah would protest their busy life-style, but more frequently she would express her irritation about some other area that she felt she had little control over.

Roger was extremely sensitive to Sarah's moods and in general masked his own feelings behind an easygoing facade. Sarah was more able to express irritation, frustration, and anger. The theme of Roger feeling responsible for Sarah's moods contributed to his expectations and growing resentment.

Therapist: As you talk about feeling resentful of Sarah's moods, I sense that part of the problem is the degree to which you feel responsible for improving them. Can we look at this together? You told me earlier that you were the closest son to your mother. Would she talk to you about some of her problems?

Roger: I don't think she really used me as a confidant for her personal problems, but she was an outspoken woman, and if she was irritated about something, everyone knew about it.

Therapist: Was it your job to try to help her fix it?

Roger: Definitely not. She was a very capable lady.

Therapist: Did she let your father help her fix things?

Roger: (laughing) No! My father was not the kind of man you would turn to to solve anything. He had his flowers and his work, but he didn't really have much to say about what was going on with the rest of the family.

Therapist: Your mother didn't seem to rely much on him to make her happy.

Roger: No. If that's what you're getting at, I was much more important to my mother than my father ever was. My mother knew that whatever I did I would do well, and she enjoyed that I was as successful as she was.

Therapist: I am sure that your mother had genuine reasons to be proud of you, but I do think that part of your need to always excel and please her was to make up in part for the disappointment she had in her marriage. Your father made your mother unhappy, but you made her feel proud and successful.

Sarah was also highly attuned to Roger's needs and ready to compromise herself in order to please him.

Therapist: You had a choice. You could have told Roger that you didn't want to go to dinner with his business friends and that you needed to spend more time with him alone.

Sarah: I can't do that right now. Four weeks ago Roger told me that he wanted a divorce. That I don't somehow measure up to the kind of wife he wants to have children with.

Therapist: You are still frightened that Roger will pursue the divorce.

Roger: I'm not thinking about it anymore. I'm not ready to say, "Let's have a family now," but I think I understand what was going wrong for me. I don't want a divorce unless we can't work out our different ideas about starting a family.

Sarah: I don't feel good about this yet. (cries for a few minutes) I still feel like I'm walking a tightrope and if I don't say or do the right thing, you'll be gone.

Therapist: Can we look at that together? You seem so frightened that Roger will just leave.

Sarah: Why shouldn't I be? My father just left.

Therapist: Can you tell me more about that?

Sarah: I don't remember very much. But I know that I loved him, and that I would have done anything for him. We had so much fun together. I know I loved him, and then one day he was gone and my mother said I would never see him again.

Therapist: Why do you think you weren't able to see him any more?

Sarah: My mother couldn't handle him being with me. I see him now for dinner sometimes, and I know . . . at least he told me that he tried every way he knew to see me. My mother felt it would be psychologically damaging to me.

Therapist: Your mother didn't want to see your father at all?

Sarah: There was another woman. She couldn't handle it.

Therapist: But your mother made it sound like she was doing this for you. That she knew what was best for you.

Sarah: That's how it always was. I ended up doing what my mother wanted, but I was told it was best for me.

Therapist: Sarah, it is not hard to imagine that a 6-year-old child would take responsibility for her father leaving. I wonder if at some level you still blame yourself for causing the divorce. It is also clear that after he left, all you had was your mother, and you couldn't take any risks in that relationship. You learned how to do what your mother wanted you to.

Sarah: I still can't say no to her. I feel sorry for her. And I think that I did somehow associate being bad with my father leaving. Do you think my mother threatened to leave me too if I didn't do what she wanted? If I wasn't a "good girl"?

Therapist: What is important is that for whatever reason, Roger makes you feel all this pain and insecurity again, and that you are afraid he will leave you, just like your father. It makes you dependent on him like you were on your mother, afraid to oppose him or disappoint him in any way. I don't see that as being helpful in the long run to either of you.

The early treatment goals focused on uncovering feelings and expectations. Both Sarah and Roger realized the importance of being able to express their feelings when they felt pressured to do something. They also realized how each needed the relationship to be perfect and how uncomfortable and frightened they were when a conflict emerged that couldn't be resolved in two minutes. Therapy provided a safe environment where specific issues could be examined more thoroughly, and the couple began to feel more confident in expressing and tolerating differences. Sarah learned to ask for reassurance when she became anxious that Roger was displeased and might leave her, and Roger learned to stand back from his initial impulse to take responsibility for making Sarah happy.

After seven or eight sessions that focused on these dynamics, the issue of children was raised.

Therapist: I think that in light of your own childhoods, the thought of having children carries a great deal of meaning.

Roger: What do you mean? I had a very happy childhood.

Therapist: One of the threads that runs through your family is the idea of loyalty. You have always been responsible and loyal to the people you love.

Roger: Commitment is very important to me. When I make a commitment I take it very seriously. I think that was what has been holding me back. Children represent a huge commitment, and I think

I was feeling under too much pressure that I didn't know how to control. I think I understand some of that better now.

Therapist: I agree fully with that, Roger, but I also wonder about commitment and Sarah.

Sarah: I am a very committed person. I haven't changed that part of me. I can say "no" better now, but I haven't stopped feeling a great deal of love for the important people in my life.

Therapist: How do you think children will fit into that for you, Sarah?

Sarah: I want a child more than I've wanted anything. Roger would be a wonderful father. I know that deep in my heart.

Therapist: What if at some level Roger thinks that you would be such a good mother that you would take over his role, too? That you might only have time for the baby? That he might be left in the garden, like his father?

Roger: That is ridiculous. I would never let that happen.

Therapist: Maybe you need to know that Sarah would never let that happen.

Sarah: I want our marriage to work more than I want children. I don't know how else I can let you know that you will always be the most important person in my life.

After this session, there was rapid improvement in the couple's ability to communicate and resolve their differences. They started to spend more time together, and the frequency and quality of their love-making improved. The couple decided to take a long vacation in Europe and saw that as the best time to terminate couples treatment. Even though both Sarah and Roger knew there were aspects of their identity and childhood that would continue to resurface and affect their relationship, their crisis was over. Roger began to complain about conflicts between therapy and his heavy work schedule and said that he had enough understanding of himself and Sarah to be able to figure out what was going on if problems arose in the future.

Sarah was ambivalent about continuing the couple's treatment, and she shared some of Roger's feelings that things were greatly improved between them and they could do well enough on their own. These issues were articulated, as were the therapist's views regarding the specific issues each needed to look at in more depth. The fears each of them might have about continuing treatment were also raised, and Roger agreed that he had no interest in discussing his relationships with his parents or other family members. The couple ultimately decided that if these issues proved to interfere with their relationship at any point in the future, they would resume treatment.

The couple called the therapist two years later for a consultation around Sarah's diagnosed infertility. Although Sarah was having difficulty sleeping and was fairly depressed, she saw the need to be in therapy as a sign that she was incompetent in yet another area of her life. Sarah displaced her anger toward the infertility specialists onto the marital therapist and decided that if the purpose of treatment was to help her calm down, then it was doomed to fail. The therapist accepted her anger and provided some support and interpretation. Sarah was quickly able to acknowledge the displacement of feelings, but she remained unable to tolerate the feelings of failure she associated with needing treatment. Roger had been the one to initiate the return to therapy, but he was able to accept and support Sarah's position. Once again, the couple prematurely terminated treatment, feeling closer, but not aware of the deeper intrapsychic issues.

Two years later, Sarah called the therapist to announce the birth of their first child. Sarah was totally immersed in loving and caring for her son, and not surprisingly, she and Roger were having intense marital conflict. Due to the therapist's impending move to a different city, the couple was referred to a colleague, and they were able to work on several of the issues that they had not been ready or able to deal with in their first marital crisis.

This couple was assessed as having severe narcissistic vulnerability, yet bringing many strengths into their treatment. From the onset they presented a need for control, reassurance, and support in order to engage in the treatment process. The problems each had with feeling controlled and the way each split self-evaluation into "all good" or "all bad" were made explicit in the early sessions. However, the couple was able to use their cognitive strengths to engage their observing egos and, with support and acceptance, they were able to tolerate and explore feelings they had formerly split off. Each was able to respond to the safety of the holding environment and to take risks in relating to the other differently.

Although important work was done on Sarah's fear of abandonment and Roger's poorly differentiated grandiose self, the major issue affecting this couple was Roger's unspoken fear of being displaced. Once the couple had expressed the importance of mutual loyalty, their intimacy was rapidly restored. The strength to recommit to this relationship was only made possible after Roger developed renewed confidence that his future was not his father's past.

Even though he was guarded against exploring his grandiose self, Roger had accepted me as a resource he could trust to "shed additional information" that could help him. Roger was pleased with the renewed marital intimacy accomplished by the short-term supportive treatment, but he was uninterested in developing greater emotional awareness and pursuing the meaning of his childhood family relations. He readily agreed to the value of treatment if there was a specific problem that affected him, but he remained reluctant to delve more deeply into his family background. Roger's resistance combined avoidance of anxiety his grandiose self could not tolerate and a value system that prized concrete accomplishments over emotional awareness.

Sarah also struggled with the protection of a grandiose self that was easily threatened. This was especially evident in her reaction to the infertility and the feelings of failure and lack of control that she could not tolerate. Her rage was intensified by facing a therapist whom she experienced as a constant reminder of her need for help and a symbol of a failure that she could not emotionally bear.

The therapist's acceptance of the couple's ambivalence and their need to remain in control allowed them to call on the therapist for help when problems eventually resurfaced. The gains that were made in the initial treatment had not been lost, despite the stresses that had emerged over time. However, the birth of a son activated unresolved issues that the couple had only superficially uncovered. It was not until they were faced with further marital conflict that the couple was able to find renewed motivation to face those aspects of their lives they would have preferred to perpetually avoid.

21 _____

Insight-Oriented
Treatment

The goals of insight-oriented therapy go beyond stabilizing the relationship. There is an expectation that each spouse is committed to understanding his or her own intimate self and how unresolved aspects of the representational world resurface in the marital relationship. The continued involvement of both spouses ensures that the marital relationship remains the focus of treatment. Each spouse benefits by deepening his or her understanding of the partner's struggles and learning how he or she can support the partner's change and growth.

Insight-oriented work cannot begin before the relationship has become somewhat stable, and it is not appropriate or possible with couples who cannot fully engage an observing ego. Couples who cannot tolerate anxiety and painful affect also need a treatment approach that is able to respond to their needs for structure and soothing more typical of the supportive or stabilizing approach.

Insight-oriented marital therapy offers an in-depth approach to conflicts that are rooted in the representational world. Issues of identity and unresolved dynamics from the family of origin are raised for exploration. Such themes as esteem, trust, dependency, responsibility, and self-assertion are examined, but within the context of the marital relationship. Both interpersonal and intrapsychic factors are considered as each spouse attempts to better understand and change their relationship in order to maximize intimacy and personal growth. Very often, spouses choose to pursue this kind of therapy through individual or concurrent treatment.

It is possible that individual psychotherapy might provide a better opportunity for the individual to achieve depth in understanding and resolving personal issues. The advantage of insight-oriented couples treatment is the frequency with which new issues emerge through the context of the couple's relationship. Projective identifications remain a valuable source of discovery regarding aspects of the representational world of each partner that come to life as intimacy progresses. Although similar issues would eventually be played out in the transference–counter-transference, or brought to the therapist's attention in other ways, the couple has already established the level of intimacy necessary to evoke material that might not otherwise be accessible. Spouses continue to be available and helpful in introducing important information that facilitates a speedier understanding of each partner's intimate self.

Case Illustration

Dana and Nancy, each in their late twenties, had lived together for two years before they sought couples treatment. Each had previously been involved in other lesbian relationships and had left their former partners in order to be together. Dana worked as a commercial artist and loved to express her creativity at home by cooking and decorating. Nancy had slowly come to feel dominated by her partner and was angry that Dana was constantly taking over for her. Conflicts would develop when Nancy started to prepare a meal, only to have Dana critique her method of chopping vegetables and insist that she could do it faster. Instead of arguing with her, Nancy would leave the room in disgust and remain cool and distanced for days. Recently the days had begun to stretch into weeks, and the couple had not made love or enjoyed each other's company for some time.

Dana had been in therapy five years earlier when she had discovered her sexual preference for women. She had some awareness of the importance of her controlling and demanding parents and her difficulty standing up to them. Nancy had never been in therapy before and was reluctant to share her feelings with a stranger. She had great difficulty verbalizing her feelings in general and was more comfortable with concrete tasks and intellectual explanations.

The Beginning Phase

Therapist: Let's see. . . . Nancy tells me that the problem is Dana's being too bossy. Dana tells me that Nancy just punishes her by withdrawing and never gives her a chance to talk things out while there is still time to solve a problem. I would say that you're both talking about power.

Nancy: Are you telling me that I have a problem with power?

Therapist: It sounds like you have a hard time standing up to Dana, and it bothers you a great deal when she has too much power or takes power away from you. I'm sure there are other aspects to this situation, but power sounds like one of them. You seem a little upset by my saying that. Do you think I'm off base?

Nancy: I have a great deal of power at my job, and I've always seen myself as being a very confident person.

Therapist: It's important to you that I also understand your strengths and how well you do in almost all the other areas of your life. Sometimes intimacy puts stress and strain on a person, and issues arise that simply don't exist in any other area of life. I'm thinking that you don't like to see yourself as having any problems. Is that so?

Nancy: Probably. I've been successful at everything I've done so far.

Therapist: It makes you angry, then, that I might accuse you of not doing something right.

Nancy: Yes.

Therapist: In some ways it sounds like I'm doing that same thing to you that you say Dana has been doing. I'm criticizing you and making you feel incompetent. The only difference is that here you stuck it out and told me that you were feeling upset. It helped me try to see things from your perspective.

Dana: I sure never get that chance.

Therapist: I wonder what made it different here?

Nancy: Well, you listened to me.

Dana: I listen to you.

Nancy: No . . . and that's what's the hardest for me. I used to think that I was special to you, but you just have your own agenda and you plug me into it. You don't really understand me at all.

Therapist: Maybe that's what we should work on first. It sounds like you have a lot of feelings about that.

Over the next few months, both were able to develop a better understanding of their ways of relating to each other. Dana was vulnerable to intense anxiety, which was precipitated by her fear that Nancy was losing interest in her. Her parents had rejected her throughout her childhood, and Dana had learned that performing in ways that pleased other people was her only way to guarantee their continued interest in her. Her attempts to take over Nancy's domestic tasks were concrete ways that she could demonstrate to Nancy how much she valued her and wanted to make her life better. They were also outlets that allowed Dana to feel accomplished and successful, as she experienced her job as repetitive and restricting.

Nancy had difficulty expressing her anger and believed that if Dana had been told once, she should be able to recognize the same problem when it surfaced again. Her style of handling anger by withdrawing was traced to her family's style of interaction, where differences could not be expressed. With support Nancy became more comfortable letting her needs be known, and Dana was able to tell her when she was anxious instead of hiding it by putting her energy into household chores.

Most of the early treatment interventions had been directed toward stabilizing the relationship. Nancy had a tendency to cling to her anger self-righteously, and her esteem was easily threatened. Dana was prone to anxiety and would explode her feelings rather than process the content and reach for a more complete understanding of herself and her relationship.

Transition to Insight-Oriented Treatment

A shift in the nature of the therapy occurred in the third month of treatment. Nancy and Dana had restored closeness and were working on being able to talk to each other about their feelings and needs. It was approaching Thanksgiving, and as we checked our calendars to reschedule the Thanksgiving appointment, it became apparent that Nancy and Dana were planning to be out of town on different days.

Therapist: (to Dana) You're not coming back until Tuesday?

Dana: Well, my sister had another baby last summer and I'd like to stay a few extra days to spend time with them.

Therapist: Nancy, why aren't you going with Dana? Do you have something important brewing at work?

Nancy: We never spend the holidays together. It just doesn't work that way.

Therapist: What happens when you try to spend the holidays together?

Dana: My family can't accept Nancy. They know that I'm a lesbian, but they don't want to know. They won't let her stay at our house, and I don't really want to push her down their throats.

Therapist: You don't want to push her or the reality of who you are?

Dana: It's the same thing.

Therapist: How do you feel about all of this, Nancy?

Nancy: I feel terrible. It's like we live with two sets of standards. Here we're a couple and we're supposed to love each other more than anything, and then Dana goes home and I'm not supposed to exist. How important can I really be to her?

Therapist: Has this been an issue between the two of you? Have you tried to talk it out together?

Dana: I guess I know that it upsets Nancy, so maybe I try not to mention it. I get very upset myself thinking about it. My parents are not understanding people. They stopped talking to me totally when I first told them I was a lesbian. For two years I didn't go home. It took my little sister's getting married to bring me back into the family, and even then it was awful. She had to cry and refuse to go ahead with the wedding if I couldn't be there. My parents were cold. It took me months of calling and just being casual for them to start treating me like part of the family again.

Therapist: Your relationship with your parents has always been on their terms.

Dana: (crying) That's probably true. It hasn't been easy for me. They're old-fashioned German people who invented new definitions of rigid. I can't even say they mean well. They don't. They're intolerant of other people and everything has to be done their way or it's wrong.

Therapist: Every time you tried to be yourself, your parents made you feel that you were wrong and not good enough.

Dana: That's why I am the way I am now, and why I would do anything to feel that Nancy really loves me.

Therapist: Dana, I think that every time you let people make you feel that you are not important or worthwhile, you believe it yourself and it really sets you back.

Dana: I have no choice.

Therapist: I think you do, but it's not going to be easy.

Dana: You mean end things with my parents again?

Therapist: Your parents sure sound like they can be difficult, but I'm not convinced that you've tried everything possible to carve out a different kind of relationship with them. I doubt if you can accomplish anything major by this Thanksgiving, but you will be spending time with them. It could be an important opportunity to look at things more carefully in terms of your relationship with them and to use our therapy to try to change how you are with them. I think this will have to be done slowly, but I think it will have important results in how you feel about yourself and how you are with Nancy. (to Nancy) Can we talk about your family and how they have accepted Dana?

Nancy: Well, it's different because my family lives here, so we never have to stay the night with them. Dana goes to her family for Christmas and Thanksgiving, but sometimes we go over to my folks' house for dinner. They were a bit standoffish at first, but I think they're polite to Dana. They always ask how she is when they call me.

Therapist: It sounds like they had an easier time accepting your choice to live with another woman.

Nancy: I don't think it's what they wanted for me or any of their children. At first they thought it was just an experiment and I'd grow out of it. But they're proud of who I am . . . proud of my accomplishments.

Over the next three months, treatment focused on Dana's work with her parents and her decision to push the issue in ways that might be easier for her parents to accept. As she put more energy into reworking her relationship with her parents, she and Nancy became increasingly close. In one session Nancy remarked that there had been a block between them before, and she was only now reaching the level of closeness she had always wanted.

In the early spring, Nancy was hospitalized for colitis. She had been in good health until this attack and was an inpatient for three weeks. She had a small portion of her bowel removed and was discharged with follow-up appointments and a specific diet. Nancy was quite depressed when she was first discharged.

Nancy: I still can't believe that my life will be different. Except when I think about the pain. I didn't know a person could hurt that bad. I could get it again anytime, and for no reason.

Dana: No. You could get it again because you eat refried beans and drink beer like you did last Thursday. And I'm not just going to sit there and watch, Nancy.

Therapist: What are you talking about, Dana?

Dana: Her diet. I know what she can eat . . . and drink. . . . I like to cook for her, but if we go out, it's no big deal. There's lots of things on the menu she can have. But she orders refried beans and drinks beer all night. And then she has hot sausage. She's trying to kill herself.

Nancy: Don't make such a big deal of it.

Therapist: I kind of think it's a big deal, too. I know you have a lot of anger inside, and I'd like to make sure you aren't taking it out on your body.

Nancy: I refuse to live like an invalid.

Therapist: You still feel like an invalid.

Nancy: (getting angry) How could you understand? You weren't in that hospital like I was!

Therapist: (gently) Go on, Nancy, tell me more about it.

Nancy: I don't want to live like this. Eat this mush. You can't have that. And you know what? It could happen again. No matter how good I've been, it could just happen again. I talked to the other patients. You know what it's like to have a colostomy? You can't slide into second base so quickly.

Therapist: Your body has always been there for you. You could use it to win at baseball and let you be part of the group. Now you can't count on it.

Nancy: I can't count on it. Me . . . the tennis star, the baseball hero. I don't belong in this world anymore. Just put me back in the hospital; that's where I belong.

Therapist: Nancy, you have a medical problem, but you will be able to adjust to it in time. We will work on your condition here.

Nancy: (screaming) My condition!! What condition? Where did you get that word? I have colitis. I have a disease inside of me, not a condition!

Therapist: (gently) You need to be able to talk about your anger. You're mad at me for making it feel worse. And you're mad at Dana for supervising you and mad at your body for getting sick. It's okay to be mad at your body for letting you down. But you are your body, and if you destroy it, you are the one to feel the pain. Your body has been something you've used before, but you've got to find a new way of accepting it as part of yourself. The hardest thing is going to be accepting something that isn't perfect, because you set very high standards for everything you have control over. And you have had control over just about everything until now. I'm here and Dana is here, and you're too smart to destroy yourself. We all have our work cut out for us now.

For the next six months, work focused on Nancy's narcissistic pain. Dana participated in most of the sessions as we talked about Nancy's way of performing in order to live up to her family's expectations. Nancy had modeled herself after her father, who was emotionally constricted and very successful in business and sports. Nancy was her father's favorite child and the son he never had. Dana could relate to the subtle pressures Nancy had responded to in order to be as successful as her family needed, and she felt that her own family had many similarities. This work was helpful in resolving Nancy's rejection of her imperfect, uncontrollable body and in helping the couple understand Nancy's sensitivity to being understood and accepted by Dana. Toward the end of the six months, Nancy started to think about the way she had established her priorities and decided that she wanted to rearrange her financial situation.

Nancy: I want Dana to quit her job. She's hated it for years. She has always wanted to own her own restaurant and cook for the world. She needs to go to cooking school, you know, to become a fancy chef.

Therapist: Well, Dana, what's your reaction to all this?

Dana: It's a dream come true. Quitting my job . . . cooking school. I just don't think it's fair to Nancy.

Therapist: You think that Nancy is trying to repay you for being there for her these past few months?

Nancy: She does, and that's not it at all. I want us to be a family. I want us to have one bank account. I want Dana to put her savings account with mine. I'll make some investments for us. We should buy a townhouse. It's crazy for me to pay rent when I make as much money as I do. And I want us to make a commitment. When Dana's restaurant is doing well, then maybe it will be my turn to quit work. But we should be working and planning together, not like roommates.

Dana: When Nancy talks like that, I get very anxious. I've never depended on anyone for years. The thought of putting my savings into a joint account makes me want to jump out of my skin.

Therapist: Your money makes you feel secure. Like you can do what you want and not have to please or depend on anyone.

Dana: I don't think I can do it. As much as I want to quit my job, I get anxious even thinking about it.

Therapist: Since I've known you, you two have slowly built a kind of relationship that neither of you has had before in your life. Each step has been hard, because it's all new, and your relationships with your parents make you doubt that you can be different. This is no exception. We'll work at it slowly and try to figure it out together.

Dana's fear of dependency was deep-seated and created intense anxiety for her. Although it seemed she was making good progress in therapy, she asked Nancy not to pressure her by raising her plan for a while. The couple started to bicker more frequently and to have passive-aggressive interactions that led to more severe fights.

Nancy: I'm really pissed off this week. I'm glad we didn't buy the townhouse. I'm not sure anymore that this relationship is going to make it.

Therapist: What happened?

Nancy: Dana doesn't want sex any more. For years she was the one who was all over me, complaining that I was distant. Well, I'm not distant any more and she doesn't really want to get close.

Therapist: Do you know what Nancy is talking about, Dana?

Dana: She's overreacting. I was tired. She can't expect me to feel affectionate every time she does. Life doesn't work that way.

Nancy: No, Dana, it's not just once. It's been like that for weeks now. You make me feel like I'm not attractive to you any more, and I don't need this.

Dana: You're putting too much pressure on me!

Nancy: And you're not listening to me!

Therapist: When things are not going well in a relationship, sex is usually the first place it shows. What you two are doing and feeling about each other outside of the bedroom is probably easiest to understand by looking at how things are going inside the bedroom. We need to talk about this together.

Dana was initially uncomfortable but gradually able to talk about her lack of sexual responsiveness to Nancy. At first she felt she was just reacting to Nancy's pressure for her to become dependent. Later, other themes emerged.

Dana: I think I'm having second thoughts about being a lesbian.

Therapist: Go on.

Dana: When Nancy came home from the hospital ... I remember this very clearly. She wanted to make love and we hadn't been together that way for over a month. Suddenly I didn't think of it as Nancy. I just started to think about another woman touching me, and it made me feel uncomfortable. I didn't say anything because Nancy was just starting to get well and I didn't want to make her upset—you know, her stitches and all.

Nancy: I can't believe you're saying this.

Dana: I'm not trying to hurt you. I'm upset by this, too. But it's important and I have to talk about it.

Therapist: You are both upset and frightened to think you might be facing something that would end your relationship. There have been so many changes in your relationship over the past year. We'll go slowly with this and see if it gets stronger, or if it's related to one of the other areas of your lives that have changed.

Over the next few months work focused on Dana's fear of closeness to Nancy, and her past in terms of her earlier hetero- and homosexual relationships. Dana discovered that her homosexuality had aided her ability to individuate from an invasive and controlling family. Even though her parents had completely rejected her for her lesbian identity, Dana had needed the expulsion in order to individuate and progress into young adulthood. Over the past year she had been somewhat successful in renegotiating her relationship with both parents, and while her father remained somewhat distant and demanding, Dana felt better accepted by and closer to her mother. Her new affiliation and acceptance from her mother caused her to question the depth of her lesbian identity and made her wish to be more like her mother and her two heterosexual sisters. Dana had previously needed to distance herself from a family engulfment that throughout her childhood and adolescence had rendered her passive and dependent. She had also split off those identifications with her parents that made her experience herself as bigoted, rigid, and uncompromising. As Dana became more aware of the affectionate and humorous side of her mother, she was able to reintegrate those aspects of her representational world again, and she became confused about her sexual identity.

Dana also became aware of how strongly Nancy's illness had affected her. When Nancy was rushed to the hospital on an emergency basis, Dana had realized how important Nancy was to her. Dana had felt totally alone and decided that if Nancy died, she would kill herself because she could never live without her. As Dana remembered and expressed these thoughts, the two were able to cry together, as they realized how vulnerable each felt for the first time in their lives. Some of the distance that Dana had been creating helped her feel less dependent on Nancy and less vulnerable to any loss. In some ways, Dana was precipitating the loss she was most fearful of.

Nancy's push to make Dana more dependent by quitting her job was also contributing toward Dana's sexual disinterest. Dana had learned not to trust objects she had to please, as she had always been forced to compromise herself in order to maintain the attachment. Despite her awareness that Nancy was different from her parents, Dana was not sure that she could allow herself to be placed in such a vulnerable position, and she continued to become anxious at the thought of losing her financial security and independence.

While Dana worked on these themes, Nancy worked on her reactions to Dana's fear of dependence. Nancy realized that she shared many of the same fears and that it was only easy for her to talk about letting Dana support her because she did not have to face that as a reality. She also became more aware of her own fears of being controlled and how alike they were in this respect. By allowing Dana to express the anxiety, Nancy could make herself feel even more poised and capable of intimacy than she truly was.

Slowly Nancy and Dana worked through these complicated themes. After another eight months of therapy, the problem was largely resolved. Dana had quit her job and had also quit cooking school after one semester. She was now making jewelry and other crafts and was showing her work at galleries. The couple had become more committed and close to each other than either had ever imagined, and Dana's sexual interest had returned with full vigor. After two-and-a-half years of therapy, it was time to talk about termination.

IV

Practice: Termination

22

Planned Termination

The termination process is an important part of any therapy, and it is often given less attention than it deserves. In marital therapy, the decision to end treatment is rarely reached at the same time by all three persons involved. It is possible for one of the spouses to feel ready to end the sessions, while the other spouse is deeply engaged in the treatment process. It is also possible for the therapist to begin thinking about the closure of treatment while one or both of the spouses are reluctant to give up the safety and improved intimacy that the marital sessions have brought about.

Planned termination refers to an ending that is thoroughly discussed and agreed upon by the therapist and the couple. Most often the couple have accomplished the goals they set out to achieve, and they are uninterested in redefining the therapy agenda to achieve deeper levels of insight. Even in extended insight-oriented treatment, there comes a time when the purpose of the sessions seems counterproductive, as when the couple are developing an unaddressed dependency or merely preserving a therapeutic relationship they have come to value.

Termination should be a time of consolidation and recognition of accomplishment. At the same time, the issues of loss inherent in any ending must be recognized and addressed. This process cannot take place adequately in one or two sessions and needs to be carefully planned and carried out.

Most couples who have had a successful treatment are aware of their ambivalence about termination. There are increasingly fewer issues to discuss in the sessions, and the couple may feel that they are wasting time and money by continuing treatment. At the same time there may be fear of regressing or losing the stability accomplished through the therapy. Couples who have been involved in long-term stabilizing treatment may additionally fear the loss of structure and the soothing and esteem-restoring functions the therapist has provided.

In termination the couple can be helped to review the course of their therapy, with particular emphasis on their progress and gains. The qualities that have formed the basis of the therapeutic alliance should also be commented upon, as most often the therapist and the couple have come to value and respect each other's personal attributes. While the couple may tend to emphasize the therapist's role in the change process, it is important that the couple be left with full realization of the enduring changes that have occurred on an intrapsychic and interpersonal level. In this way the spouses can appreciate their own growth and the new aspects of self that have been strengthened or internalized. The functions that were once delegated to the therapist have to some degree been assumed by the spouses, and the couple's ability to process and understand the marital relationship no longer depends on the proximity of the therapist. The couple who can comprehend and articulate their specific changes are enabled to leave the therapeutic relationship with confidence in their own resources.

The therapist who has successfully engaged the couple has

become a valued object to each spouse and to the couple as a system. It is not inappropriate to offer the thread of continuity by suggesting that the couple be able to contact the therapist at any point in the future should they wish to resume therapy or get input on a specific situation they might encounter. This does not replace the couple's need to end their current relationship with the therapist and to work through any transferences that may have been provoked by the ending.

Case Illustration

Saul and Fran (the couple presented in Chapter 19) were seen in conjoint marital therapy for over two years. Although the course of their therapy was neither smooth nor rapid, they had made considerable progress over that time. Fran had developed understanding into her pattern of taking care of others instead of expressing her own needs, her tendency to put on "rosy glasses" in order to concentrate on the good and ignore the bad, and her tendency to split her experiences into all good or all bad. Saul struggled to overcome his depressed moods and passivity that inevitably led to distorted expectations and resentment toward his wife. The couple's communication had improved, and they were better able to discuss their perceptions instead of making assumptions that quickly led to their destructive projective identification patterns.

The couple occasionally still used the therapist to provide structure and soothing, but Saul and Fran had begun to take over these functions with each other. Termination would not have been suggested by the therapist at this point in their treatment, but was initiated by the couple's decision to move out of state. The high cost of living in a major urban center depleted their restricted income, and as their children got older, the already cramped two-bedroom apartment seemed smaller and smaller. Fran and Saul each wanted more space for different reasons, and they agreed that they could afford a better life-style if they moved to a smaller city.

There was considerable excitement and stress created by the decision to move. The couple were preoccupied in checking out new schools, planning and executing renovations for the home they were able to buy, and helping the children prepare to leave their school friends. As the date for their departure grew closer, the therapist started to plan the exact number of remaining sessions in order to give ample time for termination.

Therapist: Well, we can count on seven or eight more sessions, but there's a lot for us to think about in terms of your ending treatment. I'd really like to focus on that today.

Saul: Not today. We're having a disagreement about the moving plans and we couldn't solve it on our own. Fran wants to take the kids and drive down a week ahead of me and let me finish packing on my own and fly down when I'm done.

Fran: That's right. I have to make a specific date with the movers, and I will not let Saul dictate when we move according to how much last-minute packing he can get done. I want to get everything booked and ready for a certain date.

Saul: And I want to be part of the family. I want to be there when the kids see the house for the first time, and we all decide how the furniture should be arranged. I want to put the kids to sleep in their new bedrooms and be part of that first day.

Fran: Then get your act together and finish your packing by the date the movers are coming. If you hadn't collected all that clutter, you wouldn't be faced with this mess now.

Therapist: I like how the two of you are saying what you each need, but I also think you've slipped backward a little. You're acting from a set of expectations that don't seem to be based on trust. I had wanted to talk about our ending the sessions today, and maybe we can look at where you're stuck and also think about it in terms of where you've been and where you're headed.

Fran: Let's just concentrate on getting us unstuck. We don't have a lot of time, and the moving company needs to confirm our exact date. I can't keep postponing them, and Saul won't talk to me if I go ahead with my plan and book them.

Therapist: You feel like Saul is being unreasonable again and that he's making it impossible for you to do what needs to be done to keep the house running.

Fran: Exactly.

Therapist: How well do you understand what Saul is trying to say? What part makes sense to you and what part doesn't?

Fran: None of it makes sense, and it's making me very resentful.

Therapist: And when you get this angry, you feel like taking over. It's an old theme—you leaving Saul out in order not to have to deal with his craziness, and kind of punishing him at the same time.

Saul: That's exactly how it feels. Like I'm going to get shut out again and treated like a bad child. I get so afraid that all of that will start over again when we get to the new home. Fran will have her space, and I'll be pushed away from the rest of the family.

Therapist: When you feel like that, it must make it more difficult to succeed with your packing. Every box you finish is a piece of reality that you're leaving.

Saul: I guess that makes sense. I've found it almost impossible to get anywhere with the packing. It just seems endless and much more complicated than I thought it would be. And Fran won't help me. She knows I need her help, and she just shakes her head. She doesn't care about how overwhelmed I am.

Therapist: And when you feel upset that Fran is ignoring you instead of helping you, it makes you cling to your plan. Do you have any idea why making a date is so important to Fran, and why she gets so upset that she can't make the plans she needs to?

Saul: She's just not thinking of me, that's all.

Therapist: You know, they say that when people leave therapy, they revert back to their old ways. Kind of their way of saying to the therapist, "We can't make it without you." Maybe it's also a way of saying, "You weren't that good. We haven't changed at all."

Saul: You're trying to be funny and this is very serious. We can't solve this on our own and we've gotten stuck in our old patterns again.

Therapist: You sure are relating to each other in old ways. But you've solved problems a lot tougher than this one lately. Why do you suppose that neither of you has been able to try to look at the other person's position and work together to figure out what's going on?

Fran: We have a lot to do. And you're wasting time with this.

Therapist: And you're angry at me. Don't you think it's all related?

Fran: I'm only angry at you because you keep wanting to talk about ending treatment, and I need to talk about getting my mover booked.

Therapist: And I won't take care of Saul for you. If I wanted, I could make him see your point, but I won't help you in the way you need me to.

Fran: That's right, and I don't know why you won't.

Therapist: You were doing fine handling these situations a few weeks ago. But you're very aware of moving, and part of that is leaving me. You've helped the kids plan how to say good-bye when school ends, but you haven't begun to say good-bye to me. You're angry that I'm not there for you right now, and I think it's an important part of saying good-bye to someone you've come to count on and depend on.

Fran: I try not to think about it. You've helped us, and I sometimes don't know how we're going to make it without you.

Therapist: Maybe if I'm not that good in your eyes, it'll be easier to let me go.

Fran: You think that that's what I'm doing?

Therapist: Partly.

Saul: I don't know what we're going to do without you either. I just know that Fran is going to turn back into her own self. There are so many complications.

Therapist: And you don't have any confidence in your own abilities to solve them.

Saul: I can't. I can't even pack.

Therapist: And I can or can't help you?

Saul: I don't think even you can help me.

Therapist: That's kind of where we started. Do you remember?

Saul: I don't think you understand how serious this is.

Therapist: I don't understand you. And I am letting you down just like everyone else you've counted on.

Saul: I don't think I'm making that up. That is what's happening.

Therapist: Yes, and it is also connected to saying good-bye to me and believing in yourself instead of counting on me to take over for you. You would prefer it if you left me seeing you as weak and you seeing me as uncaring.

Saul: Maybe.

Therapist: This issue of leaving together and your different needs in how you pack and make arrangements to go is very stressful and difficult. You two know how to work at understanding each other better, and you're not doing anything to help each other out. You are taking old stances that have always led to trouble. I think some of the anger and fear you have about not having me available for a crisis like this one is taking over your relationship and our therapy sessions. If we talk about the anger and fear, some of it is going to clear up. I have a lot of confidence in how you can end on a more positive note.

Fran and Saul were both worried about the move and what it would be like to be so far away from their therapist. Saul regressed by wanting Fran to take over for him and provoking her to punish him for his weakness. Fran became obsessed with booking the movers as a way of taking control over a move that also stimulated anxiety and uncertainty for her. Her activity also allowed her to experience a familiar, stoic self-sufficiency.

Neither Fran nor Saul found it easy to express anger or anxiety about the move to the therapist. Instead, there was an attempt to distract the therapist away from painful material and to devalue the therapist so that the loss would not feel as great. The countertransference experienced by the therapist included feelings of being overwhelmed and inadequate. It was important to define these issues and responses in order to prevent the couple from acting out their feelings and undoing the gains that had been made.

Continuing Therapy with One Spouse after the Couple Have Terminated

Planned termination is more difficult to accomplish when one partner is ready to end sessions and the other wishes to continue. It is not uncommon for one spouse to wish to pursue greater self-awareness after the marital relationship has become stabilized, while the partner is satisfied with the gains that have been made and is less motivated to continue treatment. The couple will often propose that the motivated partner be allowed to continue treatment with the couple therapist with the understanding that the spouse will resume involvement if subsequent marital problems arise.

While the couple may pressure the therapist to accept this solution, several issues should be considered before this treatment plan is agreed upon. It is possible that the couple are having difficulty accepting termination, and their plan for one spouse to stay connected to the helping figure unconsciously addresses shared fears of regression. By staying partially connected to the helpful therapist, they may be attempting to prevent any recurrences of marital distress and safeguard the gains they have made. It is also possible that the proposed treatment solution represents the splitting of functions between the couple, so that the motivated partner is formally assigned the role of carrying emotional awareness and insight for the system, while the spouse is freed from this responsibility.

While it is easy for the motivated spouse to continue a therapeutic relationship that is based on carefully developed understanding and a solid therapeutic alliance, the spouses should be made aware that it is often difficult for them to resume marital therapy with the same therapist if problems do surface later in the relationship. The therapist's impartiality will have been affected, and he or she will most likely have become a different kind of selfobject to the partner who has remained in treatment. Likewise, the spouse who has terminated therapy may have formed transferences to the therapist who continues to be an active part of his or her life through the therapy provided to the partner. While it is possible to redefine these therapeutic relationships if couples therapy needs to be resumed, it is a challenging task for both the therapist and the couple.

Case Illustration

Scott and Barbara (the couple presented in Chapter 4) were involved in couples treatment for two-and-a-half years on a conjoint basis. Throughout the couple's treatment, Barbara had remained in individual psychotherapy with an analyst she had seen on a weekly basis for seven years. During the time that the couple had been in marital treatment, they had weathered a stormy engagement, intense conflict around a last-minute prenuptial agreement, and a wedding that had started off badly and ended in a less than satisfactory honeymoon.

After the wedding, Barbara resumed her career of teaching and felt pressured for time. Even though there were many important unresolved issues, Barbara felt considerably more secure after the wedding and was less motivated to work on problems that had seemed more important to her when Scott was ambivalent about the relationship or threatening to end it. Barbara felt strongly about continuing her weekly therapy with her psychotherapist and asked for a "vacation" from the couples treatment. She agreed to resume couples sessions in six or seven months, when school would end for the summer recess and she would have more available time.

Scott, who had initially been resistant to treatment, had begun to rely on the couples therapy to help him understand his newly emerging feelings and to help him control his intense rage and need to distance from Barbara. He proposed that Barbara attend couples treatment once a month, while he would maintain weekly sessions. Although Barbara agreed, her monthly participation was compromised for a variety of unexpected last-minute emergencies and over the following four months she attended only one session. I suggested to Barbara that she come in alone to talk with me about the couple's treatment and her dwindling participation.

Therapist: I'm glad you were able to come tonight. It seems like I haven't seen you for a long time, and I've wondered how you were doing.

Barbara: Well, I'm sure Scott has filled you in on what a bitch I am.

Therapist: I know you two have done your share of fighting, but I wouldn't have put it in those words.

Barbara: Why? I'm sure Scott has you convinced that I'm the one with all the problems. He thinks the world of you, so I'm sure you're not telling him that any of this is his fault.

Therapist: Barbara, there's a lot of anger and resentment in your voice. I'm not sure you still feel that I'm on your side as much as I'm on Scott's.

Barbara: I have my own therapist who helps me feel better about myself. That's never really been your big strength.

Therapist: It's important to me to figure out what's been going on in our relationship. Do you have any idea what's making you so angry at me now?

Barbara: Well. . . . I just see you as being on Scott's side. I know what you say about our fights. Scott tells me.

Therapist: When I used to see the two of you together, you would almost always have different versions of what happened and why things went wrong. Scott used to say lots of things that would make you feel you were at fault. You haven't seen me for four months, and all that time the things that Scott has been saying have made you feel like I've ganged up with him against you.

Barbara: Yes. You only hear his side of it and he comes out of it smelling like a rose.

Therapist: And I don't care about you or your side of it anymore?

Barbara: That's right.

Therapist: Is that how you feel about me right now?

Barbara: What do you mean?

Therapist: As we sit here right now . . . just the two of us. Do you still feel like I've abandoned you and that I only care about Scott?

Barbara: I'm not sure. That's how I've felt for a long time.

Therapist: When I was not there for you to talk with, you formed a picture of me. I think a cross . . . somewhere between your father and your mother. Someone who didn't really care about you . . . who put you last. When Scott told you his version of our sessions, you probably saw me as being somewhat like Scott, too . . . demanding and unforgiving. But now I'm in front of you and I'm asking you if all those things you thought about me are what you are feeling now that you are with me, and not just the idea you had of me.

Barbara: (slowly) I guess you're not the way I was thinking about you.

Therapist: I would like it if we could try to get back some of the good feelings and trust we have developed over the years. I can remember so much sharing between us—tears and important memories that you shared with me, and times we laughed, too.

Barbara: Okay . . . when I think of that I feel like I can trust you again. But that's not how I felt after you stopped seeing me and Scott together.

Therapist: It probably wasn't a good plan. You feel like that was my fault for letting that happen. Like I should have known that you would be hurt if I let you stop?

Barbara: (tears filling her eyes) I think I only stopped because I was already feeling like you were on Scott's side. That you were more important to him than I was. He would listen to you and what you said about things, but never to me. And if you really cared about me, you would have seen that and you would have fought with me harder to stay in couple sessions. You knew I wasn't ready to stop.

Therapist: If I cared about you, I would have known what you were feeling. I would have thought more about you and what was best for you. (pause) I think that in some ways you're right . . . that I went along with the plan too easily. But I'm not sure it's right, either, for you to stay believing that if people care about you, they will do what you need them to automatically. It's always gotten you into trouble in relationships, and it sure got us into trouble, too. Some of this is your responsibility, too . . . to reach inside your own feelings and let people know that you are hurt or disappointed or that you need something different. I have not stopped caring about you, and I'd like to think that I could have responded differently if I had been given just a little more information. Maybe I felt rejected by you when you wanted to end the couple sessions, and I let you go too easily, but I never had a clue that you were feeling upset by my relationship with Scott.

Barbara: I think I didn't really understand it myself until right now.

Therapist: That makes two of us. Let's try to figure out what we can do now to fix it.

Barbara's cancellation of planned sessions was directly related to her anger at the therapist. She had terminated couples treatment because of unspoken disappointments and feelings of jealousy that she could not then articulate. Scott's continued involvement and possible idealization of the therapist had contributed to her feelings of being displaced and abandoned.

Over the months, the introject of the therapist as caring and affirming had been contaminated. Instead, the therapist was experienced as being like Barbara's unavailable parents and rejecting husband.

Once Barbara was with the therapist again, efforts were made to engage and strengthen her observing ego. Reference to positive experiences and the old therapeutic alliance helped Barbara free herself enough from the projective identifications to begin to work productively with them. Barbara needed to express her anger at being betrayed and to have these feelings accepted by the therapist before she could also consider her role in contributing to a failure in the therapy. Once the splitting was corrected, it was possible to work with restoration of the alliance and a more meaningful analysis of the events that had tran spired.

23 _____

Premature Termination

Nichols (1988) reports that the incidence of premature termination is as high as 30–40 percent. Couples frequently drop out of treatment before they have become engaged in the process and are most likely to do so when the initial sessions have raised too much anxiety or have exacerbated existing problems in the relationship. Couples may also terminate in the early phase because of their lack of fit with the personality or modality represented by the therapist.

While losing a couple in the earliest stage of treatment is not a gratifying or affirming experience, the premature terminations that are usually even more difficult for the therapist are with couples who have become engaged in treatment and who end their therapy in a unilateral decision that cannot be challenged by the therapist. Most often the therapist has failed to provide an important selfobject function or has become distorted through intense projective identifications that vividly reenact unresolved crises from the representational world. The therapist

usually experiences profound countertransference that em-
bodies the themes of rejection and abandonment evoked by the
abrupt termination. Often the therapist is left feeling helpless,
misunderstood, angry, inadequate, and/or unworthy.

The couple may announce their termination suddenly
during a session, or cancel a series of scheduled appointments.
The therapist is often able to talk to one spouse on the telephone
but cannot succeed in getting the couple to return together to
discuss their decision.

The therapist's countertransference will provide important
clues to some of the issues behind the termination. If the
therapist is provided the opportunity to process these themes
with the couple, there is some hope that the couple can be
reconnected to treatment. Often, the biggest challenge is to get
past the spouses' anger in order to get the chance to work with
them again. If phone contact is not possible, a letter can be used
to deal with the distortions and try to strengthen observing egos.
The letter or phone contact also provides a vehicle for some kind
of termination beyond the abrupt rupture created by the couple's refusal to return.

Case Illustration

William and Allison were involved in marital therapy that was
conducted on a co-therapy basis. Allison had been involved in
individual psychotherapy with one of the co-therapists and had
requested that the therapist work with her husband and her. The
therapist felt that because of Allison's boundary diffusion and strong
mistrust of strangers, he could not act as a sole marital therapist, but
he also could not successfully refer the couple for independent collateral marital work. Co-therapy provided an opportunity for Allison to
feel supported in the marital treatment and also to get the input of a
co-therapist.

The presenting problem of the relationship concerned William's
relationship with his two school-age children. William and Allison
had met at work and started an affair while William was still married.

The children had not reacted well to their parents' ensuing divorce, and they blamed Allison for the breakup of their home.

Allison was herself a child of a divorced family created through similar circumstances. She had competed to sustain her father's interest and was embittered by the postdivorce relationships she had suffered with both of her parents. Allison's feelings of guilt and her unresolved childhood pain complicated her relationship with William's children. She was also exceedingly possessive of William and fantasized that he would have reason someday to return to his wife. She felt that if she did not guard his relationships with others, he might abandon her as she had been abandoned in her past.

William felt protective of Allison and used her jealousy and possessiveness as a way to achieve differentiation from his overly involved family of origin. His parents and siblings clearly disapproved of Allison and, in response, he spent less time with them than he had before.

The couple's engagement process in the marital therapy had been drawn out and complicated as Allison had initially been wary of the "new" therapist. William had never been in therapy before and was almost entirely disconnected from his own emotional experiences. Allison's emotional agitation and tendency to explode affect had served to help him experience feelings but disown them. As therapy began to challenge his defenses, there was a time when his continued involvement seemed uncertain.

Both of these issues had been explored in terms of the couple's current way of functioning and unresolved dynamics that had been carried from their families of origin. The couple were seemingly able to get involved with the analysis of projective identifications and to become better engaged in the treatment process.

After ten weeks of therapy, the male co-therapist announced his plan to take a two-week vacation. The couple agreed to continue with the female co-therapist and to see the male co-therapist alone when the female would be on vacation the following month. In the same session there was an unusual focus on William, who had begun to process repressed feelings related to his position in his family. Toward the end of that session, Allison expressed some resentment that she had been ignored, as well as jealousy that William felt safe to share feelings with the female co-therapist but not with her.

Allison called to cancel the next marital session one hour before the scheduled time. The therapist returned her phone call during the time that was reserved for the couple.

Therapist: Allison, I just got your message that you and William couldn't make it today. What's going on?

Allison: They were supposed to deliver our new bedroom furniture yesterday, but it never got here and we had to sleep on the couch. It was awful. They said they would deliver it this morning for sure, and I'm expecting them any moment. When you called I hoped it was them saying they were on their way.

Therapist: I know you need a bed to sleep in tonight, but our session was also important. Couldn't other arrangements have been made?

Allison: Well, I have to sign for everything and tell them where to put it. I really tried to get it delivered yesterday.

Therapist: I know how these things can happen. I guess I'm trying to make sure that your reason for not coming in today is not related to the fact that M. (male co-therapist) won't be here, and you feel uncomfortable about meeting without him.

Allison: I knew he wouldn't be there when I made the appointment.

Therapist: Yes, but you might have had different feelings about it during the week.

Allison: (getting angry) I can't believe that you don't believe that my bedroom furniture is coming. Do you think I'm making this whole thing up?

Therapist: No, but I think your decision to cancel this appointment might be related to more than one thing.

Allison: Well, I'm not going to stay on the phone trying to convince you. You either take my word or you don't.

Therapist: I had to make sure there weren't other things on your mind. But now you feel like I don't believe you, and I can tell that's making you very angry. Why don't we just try to reschedule this appointment, and we can talk about it more if we need to then?

Allison: We have an appointment already set for next week. That will be fine.

Therapist: I would have preferred to see you another time this week. Do you want to think about it and talk it over with William?

Allison: Not really. But I will if you insist.

Therapist: Then you can call me sometime tomorrow. If not, I'll have to charge you for canceling today's session at such late notice. You know about our 24-hour policy.

Allison: This is an emergency and I couldn't have known about it 24 hours ago.

Therapist: I guess we're not seeing this the same way at all. Let's just leave it for the moment, and we can talk about it more thoroughly when you and William come in.

William called the next day to say that they wouldn't be able to reschedule the missed appointment and were no longer interested in couples treatment.

Therapist: I'm surprised by your decision.

William: Well, Allison was really upset by your phone call, and there's no way she's going to work with you again.

Therapist: Was it the charge for the missed session? I'm open to talking about it with both of you.

William: She was annoyed at that. But it was your not believing her about the furniture.

Therapist: I could tell that Allison was getting angry on the phone. I can understand some of it, but I also think there are other things going on now in the decision to just end therapy like this. I'm not sure that I am as suspicious and demanding as Allison feels like I am, and I'd like to think we can work it out together. Can I talk to Allison on the phone?

William: I don't think Allison would talk to you again, but I'll give her the message. Just don't be surprised if she doesn't call back.

Therapist: Where do you stand in all of this? I was your therapist, too, and I'd like to think that our work together just won't end like this.

William: Well, I've gotten a lot out of the sessions, but you don't know how upset Allison is. If I try to say your side of the story, she just gets more upset because she thinks I care more about you than her.

Therapist: I think that loyalty and people getting too close to each other is really what is going on here. The last time we met, Allison had strong feelings that I was too close to you. We didn't have time to finish talking about that. Allison also felt like you were becoming more important than her. Without M. here to balance that, I think seeing me alone might have been too much for Allison. That is at least part of what's going on, and I still think that it can be straightened out. It would make sense to make another appointment for two weeks from now, when M. is back, and Allison might feel less angry. Can I set up a time and give the two of you a chance to think more about it?

William: I will tell Allison what you said, but I'm not optimistic that she will change her mind. I can't do more than I have already tried, and I'm sure what you just said is probably true, but it won't change things.

Therapist: I appreciate your trying so hard, William. I would feel badly if things ended this way, but I guess you would, too. I'll save our ten o'clock spot and hope that the two of you will find a new way to face this kind of challenge together.

William and Allison did not return to couple treatment. Although M. tried to work with Allison in their individual sessions, she remained intensely angry. Even after the projective identifications had been addressed, Allison refused to talk with me or have a follow-up marital appointment. I wrote a letter attempting to address the need to resolve the anger, even if she didn't want to continue marital treatment.

The countertransference I experienced contained guilt and inadequacy for having contributed to the failure, and intense irritation and anger at Allison for not allowing me the opportunity to repair things. These feelings were not dissimilar to Allison's own feelings of not being treated fairly by her divorcing parents and for having in some way failed to prevent them from breaking up the family. My disappointment in William also echoed an important theme in his family of origin, where William had failed to live up to his parents' expectations.

The countertransference stimulated between the co-therapists also contained residues from Allison's representational world. Allison had achieved a victory over the rival female. The male co-therapist was now hers alone, and she had successfully taken him away from the female therapist he had initially been paired with. The male therapist remained loyal to Allison and would not abandon her in punishment, as her own father had done. Allison's consequent guilt added to her resistance to resuming couple treatment. In her individual therapy Allison was able to work through some of her feelings of fear that William had been getting too close to the female co-therapist, but she was fixed in her resolve not to talk with me again.

The co-therapists were able to address the intense feelings that had been stimulated in their own working relationship, but there was a lingering sadness and disappointment that what had started as an excellent collaboration had failed so miserably.

V

Treatment Issues

24

Conjoint versus Concurrent Treatment

There are many reasons for the marital therapist to see a couple together. It is the only way to witness and explore the meaning of the projective identification episodes that are so revealing of the nature of the intrapsychic dynamics that have been reawakened in the marital relationship. Conjoint sessions allow the therapist to directly assess the ways that the spouses relate to each other, which contributes a vital part of the overall assessment that is not available from any other source. Conjoint sessions also provide the therapist with both sides of the story so that one spouse's subjective perspective is not relied on excessively as a source of information regarding problems or progress. Spouses behave differently when they are together and elicit different countertransference phenomena from the therapist. Conjoint sessions thus provide the therapist with important clues and observations about interpersonal and intrapsychic dynamics.

From the couple's perspective, conjoint sessions ensure that each spouse is fully aware of what is going on between the therapist and spouse, and they are not made anxious by what might be said when they are not present. Often, spouses are afraid of information the partner may reveal about them. Many couples need to be seen conjointly because of fears that the therapist will take sides and no longer be impartial. This indicates a lack of trust in good objects and also a fear of being abandoned by a therapist the spouse has come to depend on. A spouse may also fantasize that the partner has developed a liaison with the therapist and may become competitive, jealous, or even paranoid about the meaning of the therapist to the partner. While these reactions clearly reveal impairments in the representational world that alert the therapist to long-term treatment goals and immediate therapeutic interventions, the reactions may be so intense that marital treatment is severely disrupted or abruptly terminated.

Conjoint treatment is important not only in assessing the couple and establishing therapeutic neutrality, but also in providing the most direct vehicle to interpersonal change. Many of the treatment goals of object relations marital treatment are best achieved through conjoint sessions. Responsive and empathic listening, for example, can only be developed through the spouses' attempts to talk together under the direction of the therapist. Conjoint sessions also provide a safe forum through which spouses can share important thoughts and feelings with each other. Even information that is addressed to the therapist is presented in the partner's presence, adding to the opportunities for each to learn more about the other. The partner's support through painful or difficult moments in therapy adds to the couple's feeling of sharing and closeness.

Conjoint sessions provide the best opportunity for the therapist to intervene directly in the marital dynamics because the therapist is able to work with immediate responses and nonverbal reactions. The therapist is able to make independent assessments regarding the impact of interventions of both spouses and to process material that may not emerge in individual sessions. Intervention in the live process is often the crux of successful marital therapy, and both spouses need to be present for this to occur.

However, there are times when it is appropriate and/or necessary to work concurrently with the spouses. Concurrent marital therapy is used here to describe separate sessions with each spouse that are conducted by the same therapist, whose focus is placed on the couple's relationship. Feldman (1992) routinely sees each spouse separately as part of the assessment and usually elects to conduct periodic concurrent sessions throughout the treatment. Nichols (1988) prefers to use conjoint marital sessions but acknowledges the need for concurrent therapy when one spouse seems ambivalent or unwilling to continue the relationship. Beavers (1985) similarly encourages concurrent sessions when there is a need to uncover information that does not seem accessible in conjoint sessions. Moultrup (1990) argues that both modalities have something unique to offer. Concurrent sessions allow the therapist to connect more firmly with the individual spouse and provide an intimacy that is productive to the treatment process. At the same time, individual sessions threaten the neutrality that is a critical component of successful marital treatment.

From an object relations perspective, concurrent sessions should be recommended when it is not possible for either or both spouses to recover a sufficient degree of observing ego to enable them to step back from their projective identifications. Spouses who become enraged to the point of losing control, or who experience severe emotional shutdown, lack sufficient ego strengths to make use of conjoint sessions (Appel 1966). Even though the therapist's understanding of a projective identification may be immeasurably enriched, a session that cannot be adequately controlled to ensure the safety of each spouse should not be allowed to continue. The therapist is also more vulnerable to accepting and acting out countertransference when the couple function on a primitive level and lack adequate self observation. The therapist's already weakened ability to provide a holding environment may be completely lost.

Concurrent sessions may also be indicated when one or both of the spouses is unable to differentiate and cannot process the relationship with independent thoughts or feelings. The spouse who is enmeshed may present defenses and symptoms that will likely diminish once some degree of differentiation has been established. The couple may need to be seen on a conjoint basis until sufficient trust has been established to allow spouses to be seen separately.

Couples who report abuse, intimidation, or violence may also need to be seen on a concurrent basis. An abused spouse who has lost the ability to regulate esteem and soothing functions may have difficulty gaining strength in the presence of the controlling or abusing partner. The existence of abuse, per se does not dictate that partners be seen concurrently. As Goldner and colleagues (1990) and Mack (1989) point out, a conjoint approach is often advantageous. The couple's ability to maintain an observing ego remains a critical factor in the decision.

Case Illustration

Penny and John (the couple presented in Chapter 4) were seen on a concurrent basis. Penny had initiated treatment and insisted that she come alone for the first appointment. Penny said that her marriage was in deep trouble, but she hesitated and expressed pessimism about whether there was any point in trying to change things. Penny didn't want a divorce and had postponed calling a therapist because she was afraid a therapist would pressure her to leave her husband.

Penny had not worked for six years and was financially dependent on John. Even though she could get a job if she chose to, she enjoyed her husband's affluence and the freedom she had to be a full-time mother to the couple's 4- and 6-year-old daughters. Penny also remembered how happy she had been with her husband when they first married, and she wanted to believe that John would change back into the man she had first fallen in love with.

Penny pinpointed much of the couple's trouble as occurring over differences regarding sex. Penny said that John would have sex with her daily if she allowed it. She described with considerable discomfort how John had acquired an extensive collection of sexual "aids" and how he would arrange different aids to be convenient for that night's activities. John would present her with some pornography and expect her to get just as excited as he was. John also liked to smoke pot and experiment with other drugs to enhance his sexual enjoyment, and Penny found herself disgusted by all of it. At the same time, Penny felt badly and inadequate that she could not be a wife in the way that John wanted her to be. She told herself that other women would be proud to have a husband who had sustained sexual desire to the degree that John had and that John was a liberated man who was honest about his sexual appetite. She also felt that John was entitled to be angry with her when she said she wasn't in the mood.

Couple treatment was recommended to Penny. Despite her initial hesitation to include her husband and her conviction that John would never come, John did agree to meet in a conjoint session. Penny had told John that she was feeling depressed and unhappy and thought things could be better between them.

John: I must admit I was originally upset when I thought about Penny wanting to see a therapist. But I have known a lot of therapists on a social basis, and think she's right that things could be better between us.

Therapist: What things come to mind when you say that things could be better?

John: Penny is a disturbed girl in a lot of ways. She is sexually inhibited almost to the point of being frigid. I know she's not always frigid, but she just won't let me help her the way she should.

Therapist: Can you respond to that, Penny?

Penny: We have a family and a lot of responsibility. I can't always be the sexy, uninhibited partner that John wants.

John: (with sudden and intense anger) How dare you accuse me of not being responsible! I carry almost all the responsibility in this family! I can't believe this conversation!

The therapist's attempts to calm John's anger and look at the distortions in communication were largely unsuccessful. As John became increasingly angry, Penny became detached and very quiet.

Therapist: John, you need to believe that Penny sees only the good parts of you. It makes it difficult when she tries to present her experiences or feelings because you hear her as putting you down or criticizing you. Can you think about how we can get past this in order to work together? Penny, I sense you're discouraged. What's going on for you?

Penny: (in a discouraged tone) When John is angry like this, it can go on for days. I can't say anything right, and everything I try just seems to make things worse.

John: I didn't come here to be put down.

Therapist: You each want to get closer and enjoy sex more with each other, but when you try to talk with each other, things get out of control. It makes it impossible for each of you to hear and use information that every couple needs in order to make fine tunings as their relationship changes over time.

Concurrent sessions were recommended. Penny agreed to talk privately again, but John would only come back with the under-standing that he saw Penny as the one who was sick. As a good husband, he was willing to see what could be done to help her.

Concurrent Sessions with Penny

In the subsequent session with Penny, the therapist's observations of her sensitivity to John's anger was explored. Penny said that John made her feel responsible for his anger, and that even though he had never hit her, she was somehow afraid that if she provoked him further, he could lose control.

John had expressed his dissatisfaction with her after the session by taking away the keys of a new car he had bought for her and making her use the old beat-up car instead. Penny was able to tentatively express some resentment at John's infantilizing treatment of her, but she became confused and disorganized when her feelings of anger began to surface.

Therapist: Penny, I may be wrong, but so much of what I see in you reminds me of other women I have worked with who are in abusing relationships with their husbands. You say John has never hit you, but I see him intimidating you in so many ways. He seems to hold all the power in the relationship, and you seem to have accepted his right to punish you for things he tells you are your fault.

Penny: (crying) I don't think I want to hear this.

Therapist: This is all new for you to think about?

Penny: People tell me how much I've changed since I married John. They say I used to be a happy, free-spirited girl. He puts me down in front of everyone. . . . It's true that I don't have any power.

Therapist: I would like to work with you to help you get some of your old self back.

Penny: I can't afford a divorce, and I don't think anyone can change John.

Therapist: You are afraid that I will take over your relationship and make you do things you don't want to. I will try very hard to just help you see things more clearly for yourself, and to help you feel better about yourself.

Concurrent Sessions with John

John had totally recovered from his anger by our next appointment but continued to insist that the focus of our conversation be Penny.

John: I always thought I was pretty good at understanding people, but sometimes I just can't read Penny.

Therapist: What makes Penny hard to understand?

John: Well, that's what I'm hoping you'll tell me. How can a wife who is so adored just turn down a husband like I'm some kind of freak? Penny can have everything in the world that I could give her. I've never met another woman like her. She's everything I've always wanted. But when I want to be affectionate. . . . Boom! She has to put me down. She's heartless.

Therapist: Are you talking about affection or sex?

John: When a husband wants to have sex with his wife, that is affection. How can two people get closer?

Therapist: When you want to have sex with your wife, that is a time when you feel strong affection. It seems you believe that if you are feeling that way, then Penny must be as well. It hurts you when she turns you away for no reason. I wonder if it's possible that she might not be feeling the same connection between affection and sex. Maybe for her affection comes before sex. Many women work like that. What do you think Penny's ideas about affection might be?

John: How could Penny not realize she is loved? Penny has got to know how much I love her!

Therapist: I'm struck by how important it is to you that Penny knows how much you love her. I'm thinking that it's just as important for you to feel loved by her.

John: That's the most important thing in my life. But how much pain can a man take?

Therapist: It's hard for you to handle all of these feelings. Penny can make you feel insecure, and that makes you uncomfortable and angry.

In the sessions that followed, Penny began to bring in material that she had previously minimized or avoided. In one session Penny described how John had humiliated her by making her believe that he had had sex with her while she was sleeping. She had awakened to find John on top of her and her genitals lubricated with jelly.

Therapist: I think this is pretty scary. How is it that you're telling me this story so calmly?

Penny: He didn't really have sex with me. I'm pretty sure. He just tried to make me believe that he had.

Therapist: It couldn't have made you feel too good about him or yourself.

Penny: It was a total turn off. I don't want him near me.

Therapist: Am I hearing just a little anger here?

Penny: Yes. . . . Now that I think of it, I can't believe I have allowed this kind of thing to happen.

Therapist: Penny, you are directing all the anger toward yourself.

Penny: Oh God. Is that what I do? Why can't I get angry at him?

Over time, Penny was able to talk about her tentative position in her family of origin. Penny's family was very religious and often criticized her for having "evil" thoughts and behaviors. She was threatened with punishments from the devil, who would take her permanently to hell. Penny's behavior was deeply affected by this threat of separation, and she became overly submissive to her parents and the authorities at her Catholic school. Penny's esteem had also been affected, and despite her beauty and popularity, she had little self-confidence. She had always been a follower who was surprised when people liked her.

Penny realized how dependent she had always been on John to do her thinking for her and to regulate her self-esteem. Her opinion of John as always knowing best became more open to modification as she started to integrate her own reality-based success in acting independently as a mother. Gradually Penny started to be able to distinguish the full range of John's feelings and behavior. She could begin to differentiate how John sometimes used sex to get close to her and how, at other times, he sought to intimidate or humiliate her. Penny began to trust her own feelings to help her understand the relationship dynamics and to begin to validate her own rights.

John vacillated between using the sessions to intellectually focus on Penny's moods and the increasing tension at home and to vent his own frustration. He would try to blame Penny for causing the increased conflict between them, but in time he was able to expand his observing ego somewhat to challenge his expectations that she would instinctively know and share his feelings. Most typically John would seem uninterested in accepting the differentiation between himself and his wife, but he would use the material discussed in the sessions in his interactions with Penny during the week. The therapist's attempts to help him connect issues of feeling controlled and insecure to his childhood were strongly resisted. John denied his problems with control, and he insisted that he simply wanted to be able to love his wife.

Therapist: When Penny talks about your attempts to get close to her, they often seem to have a lot of anger in them.

John: I'm only angry with her when she cuts me off or turns me down for no reason.

Therapist: But somehow you choose sex to express both your need for affection and your feelings of anger.

John: Well, I am angry at her. Do you know that she ripped up my pictures? (getting very emotional) She ripped them up and they were mine!

Therapist: I don't know anything about the pictures, John.

John: I took nude pictures of her when we were first married. That's almost all I have left now to remind me of how free and beautiful she is. I couldn't always have her, but I could have my pictures. She found them in my closet . . . and ripped them up. They weren't hers.

Therapist: You need to remember how special things were between you and Penny when you were first married. I can tell you are deeply upset by what she did.

John: It was the best time in my life. When I looked at those pictures, I could remember everything.

Therapist: By ripping the pictures up, Penny seemed to be telling you that those times are all over. It's hard for you to remember those good times without them, and they used to help you get through the bad times. Perhaps you are sad as well as angry.

John: They were just mine, and she had no right to hurt me like that.

Over the following six months, Penny grew more assertive in telling John what he was doing that she found objectionable and in challenging the perception that their problems were all her fault. John's first response was to move into the guest bedroom and try to lead a totally separate life from his wife. He had great difficulty accepting Penny's attempts to individuate and felt threatened and rejected. Penny was convinced that John was having an affair, and this made her more furious. John had had at least two affairs previously, but Penny had been able to deny their importance to their marital intimacy or to her personal worth. As she became more centered in her own feelings, the anger that she had repressed about John's other affairs surfaced and helped her differentiate even further from her husband.

The occasional conjoint sessions that were held ended in the expression of John's anger and resentment. Despite his discouragement, he continued to attend sessions and occasionally was able to acknowledge Penny's growing up and his need to redefine a relationship with a more independent wife. Penny became increasingly able to tolerate John's disapproval and hold her own ground when conflict surfaced.

After the couple had sustained extreme distance for several weeks, without Penny succumbing as she had typically done, John's position reversed. As he realized Penny's increased ability to function separately, he became more anxious to win back his wife's approval and affection. Penny was also able to acknowledge feelings of loneliness for her husband and regret that their relationship had gotten worse. In one conjoint session, each came prepared with a list of what they wanted most from each other, and they were able to hear each other without feeling totally criticized.

Therapy with this couple continued for over a year, with short-lived cycles of improved understanding followed by immediate regression regarding expectations and dependency. The cycle would come full circle with differentiation restored through conflict and distancing. Each time Penny and John would repeat their ambivalence about living for each other and the alternative of living without each other. Related individuation was extremely difficult to achieve. Although Penny remained more receptive to working on relationships in her family of origin, much of the time in the concurrent sessions was devoted to restoring boundaries and providing soothing for stresses that were experienced through the marital relationship.

The therapist's need to terminate treatment due to relocation caused a major setback for both Penny and John. John decided not to return to therapy and refused to take any of the recommendations the therapist had made. John denied any anger or disappointment in the therapist's leaving, and he diminished the importance of the relationship and the treatment. He left treatment resolved to live separately from his wife, convinced that all his problems with feeling rejected and controlled would disappear once he left Penny. Penny reluctantly took the names of two therapists but postponed making appointments as long as she was able to continue her concurrent sessions with the therapist. Before treatment ended, she was able to express some anger at being abandoned by the therapist and pride that she had made so many gains.

The couple was eventually able to transfer to another couples therapist, where concurrent sessions again proved useful in helping each become more accepting of and responsible for their differentiated feelings and needs.

Different Forms of Transference

The therapist who works with a couple on a concurrent basis should be aware of the nature and changes in the transference that develops. Transference exists in both individual and marital treatment but is likely to be different in the two modalities.

An empathic and emotionally available therapist quickly becomes an important nurturing and affirming object to a spouse who is being seen individually. That same spouse may seek affirmation from the therapist in a conjoint therapy context, but the therapist is triangled into an ongoing relationship and functions in a different capacity.

Because the spouses enter conjoint treatment with existing projections and externalizations that form the basis of the couple's projective identifications, the spouse is identified as the primary selfobject. Although a spouse may seek affirmation or primitive selfobject functions from the therapist, the dynamics that emerge can usually be located simultaneously in the marital relationship, and the therapist can redirect the focus in order to maintain better objectivity. The presence of both spouses helps the therapist define emerging transferences in a way that continues to place the emphasis on the couple rather than the relationship between the individual and the therapist. The transference distortions that emerge in reference to the therapist can provide meaningful information and must be addressed, but they will usually not reach the intensity they might have without the presence of the spouse.

Transference issues surface with frequency and intensity in concurrent marital therapy and may take different forms. In individuals with primitive object relations, boundaries may quickly become blurred and the therapist may be viewed as an extension of the self or the partner. If this should happen, issues that had been problematic between the spouses may suddenly get resolved or disappear, but the identical issue will surface in the relationship between the spouses and the therapist. For example, a spouse who is angry at a partner may have an impulse to end the marriage, but instead becomes angry at the therapist and attempts to terminate the therapy. More commonly, the therapist will become increasingly important to both spouses as a provider of primitive selfobject functions and may be assigned aspects of the representational world as each spouse attempts to act out internalized relationships through the projective identification process.

The changes in the relationship that result from transference distortions are important not only to the therapist and involved spouse, but also to the concurrent relationship that exists between the therapist and the partner. Conjoint sessions also stimulate intense responses in the marital partners because they fantasize about the sessions they have not attended and the nature of the relationship that may be developing between their partner and their therapist. Transference is likely to develop in the relationships both partners have with the therapist, and issues of jealousy, possessiveness, and competition frequently surface. Unresolved issues of sibling and oedipal rivalry may be easily stimulated and may provoke intense anxiety in all three members of the triangle.

A spouse will often attempt to get the therapist to comment on the partner's progress or to reveal information that was disclosed in a session he or she did not attend. This information may be abused as the spouse uses it in a distorted way to make the partner feel criticized or abandoned by the therapist. Unfortunately, the injured partner may not confront the therapist with the breach of confidence but may withdraw or retaliate in ways that are not immediately understood by the therapist.

Problems usually develop when spouses who are poorly differentiated are seen concurrently. Each spouse will be threatened by the partner's movement toward autonomy and blame the therapist for causing the anxiety and discord that often accompanies the differentiation process. Because the therapist is at the same time valued as supportive to their own development and well-being, it will be very difficult for spouses to articulate their confusion and mixed feelings. The therapist or spouse may suddenly be depreciated for reasons that cannot be readily identified.

Another common complication that accompanies concurrent sessions is the expectations each spouse may develop for the therapist to represent his or her position against the other. If the therapist has attempted to support or validate the individual needs of a spouse, he or she may expect that the therapist's role with the partner will be to reform or change the partner on his or her behalf. The spouses will inevitably compare notes and share information with each other about the concurrent sessions. When the spouse learns that the therapist has not acted on his or her behalf against the partner, he or she may feel betrayed, disappointed, or manipulated.

Case Illustration

Jeanne and Don (a couple presented in Chapter 5) were involved in conjoint therapy for over a year. Although the relationship seemed to be more stable, much of the harmony was achieved because of Jeanne's commitment to start a family and her ability to control her rage at Don's failures in order to protect the closeness necessary to accomplish a pregnancy.

When Jeanne did not get pregnant after months of trying, she initiated contact with a fertility center. Don's failure to share her concern about the infertility and his reluctance to let himself be evaluated led to an abrupt and intense rupture in the relationship. Jeanne's rage, which had been accumulating for months, was unleashed in a way that was overpowering to Don. He was unable to restore her confidence in him, and she became increasingly hostile and determined to end the marriage. At this point, concurrent sessions were recommended.

Jeanne complained bitterly about Don's absent-mindedness and his lapses in memory that she experienced as purposeful. The therapist had defined some of this behavior as passive-aggressive during the time that the couple had been seen conjointly, and Don was slowly becoming aware of how difficult it was for him to express anger directly. Don's resentment of Jeanne's demanding and controlling behavior had slowly been defined, and although he had great difficulty being angry in her presence, he was beginning to explore and experience these feelings in the therapy sessions.

Jeanne had been particularly upset one day when Don failed to meet her at the commuter train station as he had promised. When she got home after waiting for a half hour, she found him out riding his bicycle and was furious at him for forgetting about her. This incident had been discussed by both spouses in their concurrent sessions. In the following session with Jeanne, her anger was evident from our first minute together.

Jeanne: Well, I hope you think you're doing the right thing for Don.

Therapist: I'm not sure what you're talking about.

Jeanne: Don't play innocent. You know I'm talking about the session you had with him last week.

Therapist: Well, I can see you're very angry about it, but I'm not sure why.

Jeanne: Look, I know what you said to him. You're entirely two-faced. You meet with me and you're so sympathetic. You "understand" exactly how I feel waiting at that stupid station, and you understand why I feel like it was all on purpose.

Therapist: Yes, I could really imagine how you felt that day.

Jeanne: Great. Then you meet with Don, and what do you tell him? That he had been upset with me for putting him down the night before. And you feel so sorry for him. Poor baby, his wife criticized him in front of his friends, and he had tried so-o-o-o hard to be a perfect husband. He's walking all over you. Do you think he's ever going to change when all you can do is help him feel sorry for himself? I was the one left at the station.

Therapist: You wanted me to be different. Maybe to be angry at Don like you were and tell him how wrong he had been?

Jeanne: Of course. That's what you led me to believe. You meet with me and you take my side. Then you meet with him and you just take his side. You can't take both sides. Don't you know where you stand?

Therapist: Jeanne, I think the things that Don does to make you angry are related to other things that have recently happened. I know you wish I could just lecture Don and make him change, but the truth is that Don has to find his own voice. What I also think is that you are angry at me because I've let you down, and there are important things going on in terms of whether you can depend on me to take your side.

Jeanne: What is going on is that you want both of us to like you, and you are letting Don walk all over you. I can't believe that you think he will ever change unless you tell him how sick he is.

Therapist: You see this as being all Don's fault, and I see this as being interactive. If I say that part of why this happens is how you and Don get along when you are being tough on him, then you get very angry at me. But I would no more tell you to quit yelling at Don than I would tell him to quit forgetting things important to you. I just don't think it works that way.

Jeanne: Well, when you take his side, you aren't helping things.

Therapist: When you see me as taking his side, then you think I'm making things worse for you and that I can't be trusted. Don't you think that sounds familiar in light of how your mother used to treat you when you were little? She would pretend to be your friend and then turn on you or put you down when you least expected it?

Jeanne: I think you're changing the subject.

Therapist: I think you're still mad at me. And unless you think you can control what I do with Don, it makes it impossible for you to let me work with each of you in the way that I think is best.

Jeanne: I still think what you're doing is wrong.

Therapist: This boils down to confidence in me. I have every belief that if I did exactly what you wanted me to do, it would end in disaster for both Don and you. I can understand your wish, but I can't go along with your plan. I am taking a stand and not trying to please you, but it's not what you want from me, and I think it makes it harder for you to trust me.

Jeanne: I guess you know what you're doing. But when the two of us get together and find out what you said to the other, it just blows us away.

Therapist: You see me as taking the easy way out by agreeing with each of you. The truth is, I do think each of you has a point.

Jeanne: Well, maybe we each do things wrong. But you're just too nice to Don, and he thinks you're giving him permission to do these shitty things to me.

Therapist: Well, that's a mistake on my end, then. I am trying to help Don understand where these things come from so he doesn't need to do them any more, not so he will keep on doing them.

Jeanne: Well, just make sure that he sees that part. I will not be the one who is blamed for being left at the train station.

Therapist: I can see how it looks that way, and I know you feel that's completely unfair. Can we look at that more carefully together?

Jeanne had at some level blamed me for the fact that their marriage had not been "cured" during their first year of therapy. Her dreams of having the ideal marriage and making a perfect baby had been suddenly taken away from her. Jeanne had difficulty letting go of control before her marital crisis, and her mistrust of others had been intensified by her experiences of having an imperfect husband and an imperfect therapist.

Jeanne was ineffectual in making Don change and saw the therapist as a potential extension of herself who could help her change Don in the ways she dictated. When the therapist would not be controlled, Jeanne became enraged. Jeanne experienced the therapist's support of Don as betrayal. There were also elements of possessiveness and competition, as Jeanne was distressed by the therapist's apparent concern for Don's well-being in a situation that Jeanne felt had been traumatic only to her.

Jeanne was often engulfed by her anger and had difficulty reestablishing a therapeutic alliance because of the transference distortions. A holding environment was created wherein Jeanne's anger could be accepted but redefined by the therapist. Unfortunately, the interpretation of projective identifications rarely succeeded in defusing Jeanne's feelings. It was equally important for the therapist to demonstrate that Jeanne's anger would not demolish the therapist's availability to her or lead to retaliation. Only through this repeated testing could the alliance slowly be strengthened and eventually provide enough safety to free Jeanne from the anger fueled by her lack of omnipotence.

Secrets

The use of concurrent sessions raises other treatment challenges that need to be anticipated and responded to quickly by the therapist. The most common issue is the therapist's response to secret information that is revealed with the expectation that it will not be shared with the spouse. Commonly, this pertains to the existence of an affair or plans to end the relationship. Other secrets may involve information about bisexuality, finances, or facts about the individual's past that he or she wishes to keep secret from the spouse. Very often this information is revealed before the spouse and therapist have reached a mutual decision regarding secrets and the therapist's role in preserving the secrecy.

The topic of secrets has been addressed by several theorists, as it raises issues of confidentiality, impartiality, legal obligation, and ethical responsibility (Kantor and Kupferman 1985, Moultrup 1990). All of these concerns should be thoughtfully considered before the therapist is confronted with the clinical issue and an immediate response is required.

From an object relations perspective, the secret activates a coalition that allows for a repetition of internalized dynamics from the representational world. The spouse may be trying to seek the support and strength of an affirming good object or undo the experience of being judged or blamed from a projected critical superego introject. It is also possible that the therapist will be responded to as a weakened, ineffectual accomplice and subsequently carry the split-off negative self representations. By sharing the secret and immobilizing the therapist, the spouse may begin to act toward his or her partner in a punitive or demeaning way and feel supported in this by the therapist who is protecting the secret.

The impact of the secret on the partner should also be considered. The secret forces an alliance that makes the therapist less powerful but more engaged with the "revealing" spouse. The status of the partner is automatically changed, and the therapist is frequently stimulated to carry a response that has been split off from the spouse who revealed the secret. In many instances the therapist may experience a countertransference of protectiveness toward the "unsuspecting, innocent" spouse. If the therapist acts out this countertransference with the couple, then the revealing spouse is further free to express the rejecting punitive spectrum of the ambivalence. The therapist may also act out countertransference by casually trying to alert the innocent spouse that all is not well and to become more suspicious or watchful. In all of these scenarios, the impartiality and effectiveness of the therapist is severely compromised. If this happens, it is often advisable for the therapist to confront the impact of the secret on the couple's treatment with the spouse who has created the complication. If the spouse refuses to share the secret, the couple may need to be referred elsewhere.

Case Illustration

After several months of concurrent marital therapy, Jeanne started to have an affair. The romance with C. started on a business trip when the two went for dinner and Jeanne discovered she had a sympathetic and attentive friend. Jeanne had been discouraged by the lack of improvement in her marriage and was relieved to meet a man who could listen to her with genuine and sustained interest. Jeanne initially minimized the sexual aspects of this relationship, but ultimately she came to value the lovemaking and her ability to respond to a man in a way that she had not reached with Don.

Jeanne had initially refused to tell Don about the affair but had grown more distant from him and started talking about separating. Don was at first upset by Jeanne's threats to separate but had quickly convinced himself that she was simply doing this to make him angry. Don would avoid and minimize the marital discord and tried to divert the therapist's attention into helping him deal with stressful situations at work. As the weeks went by, therapy with Don became increasingly uncomfortable for the therapist. A decision was made to confront Jeanne with her avoidance of the situation.

Therapist: Jeanne, it's been three weeks now that I've been telling you that you have to tell Don what's going on, and three weeks that Don doesn't seem to know anything.

Jeanne: I try to tell him, but he doesn't hear me. It's really the story of our relationship—he doesn't hear.

Therapist: Tell me more about how you tried to tell him this week.

Jeanne: I told him that I felt very distant from him and that I felt better sharing my feelings with a business colleague in Pittsburgh than I did with him.

Therapist: What did he say?

Jeanne: It's ridiculous. He's convinced that I'm just jealous because his secretary asked him out for drinks and that I'm just saying these things to get back at him.

Therapist: I think that Don is finding ways not to hear things that might upset him too much. But you aren't exactly making them crystal clear either.

Jeanne: He's never gotten it. Nothing ever gets through. He's dense. I've always had to spell things out for him and I'm sick of it.

Therapist: In a way you're trying to make him responsible for your starting this affair and now for your continuing it without his knowledge.

Jeanne: You have no right to say that to me. You're trying to make me feel guilty.

Therapist: If I don't talk to you about what you are doing in your relationship, then I'm joining you in giving you permission to do what you want because it wasn't your fault. If I don't go along with that, then you see me as being the disapproving Puritan who is condemning you. Don't you think that you also carry those feelings about yourself, but it is easier to see it as just coming from me?

Jeanne: I've told Don I'm thinking about separating. I've been complaining about our relationship for months and months. That's not exactly withholding.

Therapist: When anyone has an affair, they're saying important things about their marriage. You are not being valued or listened to in your marriage. Your attraction to a man who can provide that for you stresses how much you need those things. You've been thinking about separating. But having a lover who makes you feel secure would make that seem so much easier. The only problem is that I think there is still a part of you that isn't ready to lose Don.

Jeanne: That's right. I'm saying separation, not divorce. But he still doesn't think I'm serious.

Therapist: Don is burying his head in the sand because he's afraid of losing you. That means that he can't hear anything that you tell him and he can't give you the things that you need the most. If you really want to save this marriage or if you even want to find out whether Don is capable of responding to your needs, you have to let him know what's going on. I told you last week that you can't work on a marriage and an affair at the same time. You've learned a lot about what you need from a man. There's no way you can sustain two relationships like this for very long.

Jeanne: You're lecturing me again.

Therapist: You hear me as being critical. Let me think about that this week. Maybe at some level I am. What's getting hard for me is seeing Don when he has no idea of this affair. I feel like prodding him to pay more attention to you and what you are doing—trying to push his head out of the sand. But that's not my job, Jeanne, and it interferes with my ability to be truly impartial. I can't let myself take over telling Don and changing him for you, and I can't be your critical mother who won't let you enjoy life. That's how this is starting to turn out, and the longer it goes on, the more ineffectual I get. Maybe that makes me easier for you to be with, but it's not allowing you to get very good therapy. I don't want to work with my hands tied, and I think we should set up a session for the two of you to come in together. If you haven't told Don before then, we'll use that time to try to turn this around.

Jeanne: Well, I think you're just going to end up hurting him.

Therapist: Jeanne, I think that's the part of you that isn't ready to end your marriage. Part of you cares for Don and doesn't want to hurt him. You think that I am the one trying to hurt him now.

Jeanne: Well, it gets confusing for me. I want him to change but I don't want to hurt him. Or maybe I do.

Therapist: Maybe there is also a part of you that's feeling frightened and guilty.

Jeanne: I guess both. This marriage didn't exactly work out the way I had hoped.

Therapist: Sometimes you see this marriage as being hopeless and all bad.

Jeanne: I guess I do. And now I've made it so bad it can't be fixed.

Therapist: I can understand how you feel that. You were angry and needy when you met C. And doing something bad was all this marriage deserved. But there are times when you remember the loving parts and the good times, and then you don't know what an affair would do to that good part.

Jeanne: (sadly) Part of me still does love Don, and I don't want him to know about the affair. I've really made a mess of this.

Because of the extent of the splitting, Jeanne experienced the marriage as all good or all bad. When she was angry and disappointed, she could engage in the affair and feel justified and provoked. When she was confronted with the loving side of Don, she became overwhelmed with guilt and fear and tried to deny that the affair existed. Don's avoidance made it easier for Jeanne to feel that she had done everything possible and that it was his fault the affair was continuing without his knowledge.

Jeanne stimulated the therapist to feel critical and disapproving and to carry her own punitive superego introjects for her. The therapist was also provoked to accept Jeanne's former role of explaining things to Don and, in that way, take care of him. Had the therapist accepted the projective identification, then Jeanne would have been ultimately punished by a therapist who would reject her in order to take care of her spouse. Jeanne also would have been contemptuous toward an ineffectual therapist and would have displaced her self-disappointment onto a therapist who had failed to live up to her expectations.

These dynamics provided important clues into Jeanne's representational world and needed to be processed in order to contain her acting out. The secret would have changed the therapist in ways that would have allowed Jeanne to reenact earlier trauma but, like the marriage, would have destroyed the marital treatment beyond repair.

Therapeutic Precautions

In order to prevent these complications from contaminating the marital treatment, it is important for the therapist to try to connect with each spouse on an individual basis and to establish as strong a therapeutic alliance as possible. When projective identifications emerge, it is critical that the therapist be able to use the relationship to restore and strengthen the observing ego and use the distorted reaction in a productive way to help the spouse learn about his or her own split-off issues. It is also important that the therapist be particularly watchful for countertransference and use any changes in self to assess the unfolding marital dynamics.

In order to recognize and deal with complications that may be unfolding in the marital relationship, concurrent treatment should include occasional conjoint sessions. This is important in allowing the therapist to observe directly any changes in the dynamics that are being focused on in the concurrent sessions and to gain further understanding in the unfolding projective identifications. It is also the best way to identify problems that may be the result of secrets, unidentified transferences, and problems with jealousy and competition.

Concurrent sessions may be necessary, but the modality carries sufficient risks and inherent problems that it should be used judiciously. As the spouses become better able to maintain differentiation and sustain an observing ego in each other's presence, the balance of conjoint and concurrent sessions should shift, so that ultimately the couple will be able to work predominantly on a conjoint basis.

25 _____

Collateral Marital Treatment

It is not uncommon for marital treatment to begin while one or both of the spouses is involved in individual psychotherapy. It is also possible for a marital therapist to refer one spouse for concurrent individual treatment in the hope that he or she will pursue important individual issues that cannot be responded to in sufficient depth within the framework of conjoint marital treatment. The situation can develop where two or three therapists who work independently and from different perspectives impact on the marital system simultaneously.

The consequences of multiple, independent therapists working with the same couple should be thoughtfully considered, whether the role is to provide collateral marital treatment to the couple or collateral individual treatment to one of the spouses. Braverman (1985) suggests that marital treatment is usually sought when the spouses in individual treatment have reached an impasse, which is usually caused by projective identifications that cannot be disrupted through individual treatment. She recommends that marital treatment always be brief, as there is a strong risk that the marital therapist will be seen by one or both of the spouses as the bad object. Braverman recommends that the marital treatment should not aim for insight but should provide behavioral interventions that reveal the projective identifications in such a way that the spouses are forced to take responsibility for their parts in the collusion.

Individuals who use splitting as the predominant defense mechanism do tend to relate to their therapists as primitive selfobjects. Because the individual therapists have taken over critical psychic functions, there is usually some degree of merger, dependency, and transference of good and bad internalized representations. This operates not only for the spouses who are in treatment but for their partners, who also fantasize and project material onto the omnipotent authorities they may have never met, but who strongly influence their spouses and their intimacy.

The Reenactment of Internalized Dynamics through the Therapists

Very often, a complex drama created from internalized representations becomes reenacted through the therapists, who, through countertransference, are stimulated to act out specific roles. This phenomenon has been noted on psychiatric wards, where disturbed patients commonly provoke the professional staff into acting out against each other (Lansky 1981b). The dynamic has also been noted in co-therapy, where at different times each co-therapist is viewed in polarized ways and often induced to act out the couple's issues with each other. The difference between these therapy situations and collateral treatment is the frequency and nature of contact among the therapists. Even though a collateral therapist may never have met or talked with a primary therapist, it is indeed possible for the spouse's internalized object relations to be reenacted with amazing intensity and accuracy.

Case Illustration

Pam and Neil, each in their early thirties, had been involved in individual psychotherapy when they sought couple treatment. Neil had been in treatment for four years because of an obsessive compulsive disorder with situational anxiety and phobias. Pam, who was finishing a degree in psychology, was just terminating supportive psychotherapy, which she had sought to help her deal with the reactive stress of moving to a new city and unanticipated relationship complications.

Pam and Neil had been involved in a long-distance romance for two years and had grown increasingly committed to each other. Pam moved in with Neil two years previously and took a part-time job while she finished her dissertation. The couple expected to announce their engagement after a brief trial of living together.

Things had not gone well and, as Pam put pressure on Neil to announce their engagement, he became increasingly anxious. Neil became fearful that Pam might become pregnant, and his anxiety turned into a phobia of intercourse with anticipatory anxiety and avoidance.

Neil opposed the marital therapist's suggestion to speak directly with his psychotherapist, with whom there had been no previous contact. He described his psychotherapy as private and as something he needed to feel in control of. Pam expressed feelings of resentment and jealousy toward Neil's therapist. She felt that she had always come second and that when something special happened to Neil, or if he had important feelings, he told his therapist before he told her. She believed that Neil's therapist was "against" her, and she had actively tried to discourage Neil from getting close to her. She blamed the therapist for making Neil break their engagement instead of supporting him to grow in his personal life. Because the therapist was a single female, Pam fantasized that she was romantically interested in Neil herself and that she was sabotaging Neil's romance.

Couple therapy focused on the projective identifications each brought into the relationship. After two or three months of weekly sessions, the couples therapist learned that Neil was abusing large amounts of Valium that he obtained through prescriptions from an internist recommended by his psychotherapist and medication that his mother's doctor supplied him with. Neil had manipulated the situation so that each source was unaware of the other and the total amount of Valium that he was consuming. Rather than allow the marital therapist to share this information directly with his psychotherapist, Neil agreed to tell her about his drug manipulation himself. The marital therapist encouraged Neil to be assessed for medication at an anxiety disorder clinic of a well-known teaching hospital, where he could also get proper psychiatric/medical supervision withdrawing from his addiction.

Neil stimulated intense countertransference, which was acted out in the relationship between the couple's therapist and his individual psychotherapist. Each perceived the other as somewhat incompetent in allowing Neil's problems to develop. There was a competitive dynamic between the therapists, as each felt she had the best plan for Neil and saw the other as being an impediment.

When the extent of the countertransference unfolded, the marital therapist confronted Neil.

Therapist: What's happening with the Valium?

Neil: My therapist was disappointed in me, but she said that different people have different tolerance levels to Valium. She is going to help me reduce my dependency, and she doesn't think that involving any more therapists or doctors is a good plan for me right now. I think I like your idea of the anxiety disorder clinic better, but maybe I can stick with her plan for a month or so, and if it's not working for me, we can go ahead with that referral like you want.

Therapist: (aware of feeling rejected, annoyed at Neil's psychotherapist, and having an urge to try to convince Neil to follow her plan sooner) It seems like you're in the middle here between two people who want the best for you, but have different ideas of what that means. I sense you are doing your best to keep both of us happy and to please us both. It raises issues of loyalty and competition. You're doing a great job of juggling; I bet this situation is not new to you. Can we look at it together?

    Neil: Well, I like both of you, and I can tell you are each very knowledgeable.

    Therapist: For the moment I was thinking more about your parents. Did they work well together on your behalf?

    Neil: No. They're each strong-willed, and they have very different ideas about life.

    Therapist: Can you tell me more about that?

    Neil: I guess I was always trying to please my father most. He was interested in sports, and my brother was a natural athlete. I would practice and practice in order to beat my brother, but somehow my brother always looked better, and my father always had something great to say about him.

    Therapist: You needed to please your father, but no matter how hard you tried you weren't made to feel good enough. How does your mother fit into this?

    Neil: Well, I was always smarter than my brother, and my mother was very proud of my grades. She would tell me that school was much more important than baseball, and she would talk to my father about putting less pressure on me.

    Therapist: Would they agree?

    Neil: No! My parents would get into huge fights about what was best for me. It was awful.

    Therapist: Each of your parents wanted something from you. You tried hard to please both, but you also had a lot of anger and resentment. Somehow you would find yourself in the middle of two strong people who were fighting with each other about you. Each one could express anger at the other for you, so you never needed to be angry or express your own feelings for yourself. I see that happening again now . . . between me and your therapist, and between your therapist and Pam. Everyone who cares about you ends up expressing resentment toward the other people in your life and competing to be your favorite. Instead of feeling like you have to compete all the time, you get other people to feel the need to compete for you.

Collateral Treatment of One Spouse

Collateral treatment may be also be initiated by the therapist who is treating the couple. In this situation, the couple's therapist is aware of issues that require more attention than can be provided through conjoint or concurrent sessions. Individual psychotherapy for one of the spouses is recommended in order to help that spouse deal with important intrapsychic matters that will ultimately benefit the couple's relationship.

It is important that the individual and couple therapist be able to discuss the referral in depth. The couple therapist's expectations and understanding of the interpersonal and intrapsychic issues must be thoroughly understood in order to maximize treatment and avoid countertransferential acting out. This is especially important when the spouse referred for psychotherapy has primitive internalized object relations. The tendency for these spouses to use excessive splitting will lead them to relate to their therapists alternately as all good or all bad. Therapists who are able to communicate with each other throughout the treatment are better able to use this in a therapeutically helpful way and avoid the kind of acting out that was illustrated in the preceding case example.

As the psychotherapy begins to effect change and increased awareness in the spouse, there is usually a shift in the relationship dynamics. Usually, the projective identification patterns are exposed in greater depth at a faster pace. This does not always result in an improved relationship, and there may be intense turbulence as one spouse begins to react in ways that contradict long-established patterns that have maintained the couple's homeostasis.

Case Illustration

Anna and Doug had sought help at a sexual dysfunction clinic and had been seen in couples treatment for six months. The presenting complaint was Anna's inability to experience orgasm and her avoidance of sexual relations. The couple was in their early fifties and had two grown children. Anna was closely connected to her family of origin and assumed responsibility for the overall well-being of her parents, who lived in a nearby town.

Anna had no formal education and had been struggling to define a role for herself since her children left home. She worked part-time as a home cleaner, and although she enjoyed earning money, she was embarrassed by her vocation. Anna avoided socializing and believed that others would not find her interesting or important enough to spend time with.

Anna was very subservient to her husband, who was a successful foreman at an engineering plant. She also made herself excessively available to her son and did his laundry, cleaning, and shopping. Anna had little emotional insight, but was motivated to make changes in her life. She was afraid to drive her car in bad weather and was easily intimidated by other people. Anna was also alexithymic, and instead of expressing anger, she would be immobilized by severe headaches and back problems.

The couple's therapist thought that Anna needed support in the separation-individuation process and could better become less submissive and reliant upon her husband if her self-esteem was improved. He also thought that she would be freer to discuss her sensuality with a female therapist and that these issues could not be accomplished in the conjoint marital sessions.

Anna, who had a Spartan, masculine appearance, was initially compliant and deferential. She hoped the therapist could tell her how to handle certain situations and asked for concrete recommendations. As therapy progressed, she became more able to present her viewpoint and, gradually, to articulate feelings.

Doug enjoyed nude sunbathing and each weekend, in the warm weather, the couple had gone to a private nudist colony. Although Anna denied being uncomfortable with this life-style, she expressed a wish that just sometimes they could do something different—something that she wanted.

Therapist: What kinds of things do you wish you were doing together?

Anna: This is probably silly, but I'd really like us to go to the zoo . . . maybe have a picnic there and just be with the animals.

Therapist: It sounds like a lovely day. What happens when you think of asking Doug to go there with you instead of the beach?

Anna: (shyly) I wouldn't know how to do it really. He works so hard during the week, and he would make me feel like I was taking something away from him.

Therapist: It's hard for you to think that your needs could be important or that Doug should have to make compromises in order to make you happy. Do you think that just goes on between you and Doug, or is that the way you are with other people in your family?

Anna: I've always tried to make other people happy.

Therapist: Can we talk about what it was like for you growing up? I know that there were six kids, but you weren't the eldest. . . . Weren't you right in the middle?

Anna: I was in the middle, but my eldest sister was smart and beautiful, and she did real well at school. My brother wasn't as smart as her, but he was a lot smarter than me.

Therapist: You don't think you were very smart. I can tell that's very important to you.

Anna: (starting to cry) I never failed a grade. I almost did once, but I worked very hard to get my grades up. I always had to study so hard, every night, but I just couldn't get good grades.

Therapist: How did your parents react?

Anna: My mother said I was just like her and I never would amount to anything. She said I should just learn to get along with others and not try so hard to do what I couldn't do anyway.

Therapist: That's a really mixed message.

Anna: She was trying to help me feel better about myself.

Therapist: And did you?

Anna: No. I still don't either.

Therapist: To you, being smart and getting along with other people and having self-respect are all jumbled up together.

Anna: Well, shouldn't they be? What right do I have when I'm so dumb?

Therapist: I don't believe for one moment that you're dumb. And I think that you have let other people define who you are for too long. I wonder if you are really like your mother, or whether it was something your family wanted to believe? I would like us to figure that out together.

Anna: You really don't think that I'm dumb?

Therapist: You are one of the bravest women I know in terms of how many risks you have taken in your therapy. You understand things and observe things about yourself and other people that really impress me. I don't know how you did in school when you were a little girl, but I think you're smart.

Anna: (crying again) I wish I could feel that way about myself.

Therapist: I wish you could, too. Last week you felt very proud of how you handled that rude saleswoman. Maybe there's a part of you that does like yourself sometimes now.

Anna: I think there is. I don't let myself feel that very often, though.

Therapist: Why do you think that happens?

Anna: I guess I believe what my mother told me. I shouldn't get too big for my britches. If people don't like me then I won't. . . . I don't know exactly.

Therapist: It's hard to put it in words.

Anna: It's like I know that something bad would happen but I don't know what.

Therapist: Are you brave enough to find out?

Anna: You mean what would happen if I let myself stay feeling good about myself and that what I wanted might be a good idea?

Therapist: How does that sound to you?

Anna: Scary, but exciting.

Anna did confront Doug with her wish to spend a day at the zoo. This became an important subject in the couple's treatment, and the couple began to explore their distribution of power. Both Anna and Doug took responsibility for opening new doors for each other, and as Anna became more assertive in expressing her viewpoint, Doug was able to explore his own insecurities in being challenged.

Later in the individual therapy Anna wanted to talk about sex. She and Doug had been involved in progressive touch exercises, and she had enjoyed being massaged but still didn't feel like having sexual intercourse.

Anna: I know that Doug thinks I'm attractive, but I don't feel sexy.

Therapist: What does that mean to you . . . sexy?

Anna: You know, being a cover girl or wearing garter belts.

Therapist: How do you suppose you got those ideas about being sexy?

Anna: Well, that's what Doug wants me to do. He's bought that stuff for me to wear, garters and sexy nightgowns. But I put them on and I feel silly and not like me.

Therapist: Having sex with Doug when you feel uncomfortable or awful about yourself couldn't feel very good.

Anna: It doesn't.

Therapist: Pleasing Doug, but letting yourself feel humiliated isn't what sex is all about.

Anna: I could do better now saying no if I didn't want it to go further.

Therapist: That is important. But I sense that you're looking for something more. . . . Maybe a way of enjoying sex more for yourself, and not having to say no as your only option and ending it there for both of you.

Anna: That would be new for me . . . enjoying sex. And Doug wants to please me. . . . He would do anything. It's just me. I can't relax and let myself go.

Therapist: There are two important things going on for you. One is feeling sensuous for yourself, letting yourself feel and experience yourself as sexy. The other thing is trusting Doug or trusting yourself that it would be okay to let go. You've told me you can have an orgasm by touching yourself, but somehow it feels different to let that happen when Doug is with you. Why don't we work together on the first part . . . about feeling like a sexy woman, and you take that second part about trusting Doug into your couple sessions.

Anna: I don't want to feel cheap.

Therapist: Anna, all these years you have been making important observations for yourself about what is and isn't attractive in women. When you look at a magazine, you admire certain models and you turn your nose up at others. I think you have lots of ideas of what makes a woman beautiful and desirable, but you haven't given yourself permission to use those ideas on yourself.

Anna: I guess I've always just seen myself as a mother, you know, too old for that kind of thing.

Therapist: And maybe not important enough. Some of the things might mean spending money. But some of them are ideas, fantasies about yourself that you can use any time you want. I have noticed how creative you are in planning parties or doing things for the house . . . but not for yourself.

Anna: I think I get what you mean. I do have ideas about what is beautiful and how I wish I was. It's just like everything else. . . . I've been putting myself last and being afraid to take chances or live my life. I can't live my life through other people any longer. I am not my mother!

Over the next month there was a dramatic change in Anna. She had her hair cut in a fashionable salon and began to wear attractive earrings and scarves. She giggled when I commented on her changing appearance and said she had no idea how much fun it would be. Anna was experimenting with her sensuality and for the first time in her life was able to express and verify the attractive, feminine aspects of herself.

Although Doug was initially receptive to these changes, the couple's therapist reported that as Anna became more interested in sex and achieving orgasm for herself instead of pleasing her husband, Doug developed impotence. The couple realized for the first time that competency and self-esteem were shared problems, and that for years Anna had carried the worthless qualities for both of them. When Anna became more sexually playful and confident, Doug became inadequate and depressed. It was not until these areas were addressed in therapy that his sexual health returned.

Anna had accepted an identity as helpless and inadequate from her family of origin. She had put others above her throughout her life and used self-sacrifice as a way of maintaining attachments to the objects she was dependent upon. These dynamics were perpetuated in her marriage and in her relationships with her adult children. The concurrent individual sessions allowed Anna to focus on those aspects of self that needed to be developed and supported before she could become more assertive in defining herself differently with others.

26 _____

Reaching the Couple through Family or Individual Therapy

Not all couples who have marital problems locate the source of their conflict and stress as stemming from the marital relationship. It is not uncommon for spouses to define the cause of their unhappiness to be a problematic child. It is also possible for the spouses to redefine the problem as being located entirely within one spouse, as evidenced by psychiatric symptoms (Hafner 1986). In these instances, the couple is often attempting to preserve the experience of the dyad as all good. In order to ensure the safety of the marriage, the spouses must deny or avoid the conflicts and disappointments that, for the moment, seem too overwhelming to be conquered. The therapist should appreciate the reasons that perpetuate this defensive posture but move as quickly as possible to work directly with the marital relationship.

Triangled Children

Very often marital conflict is displaced onto the children, who act out the issues for their parents. Although these parents are able to seek and accept help because of their children's problems, the spouses are often resistant to examining their own relationship. It is not until the children have been released from the family triangle that the full-blown problem in the couple's relationship emerges. At this point, the therapist has to help the couple make the transition from family treatment to couple treatment and focus on a relationship that has long been avoided and neglected.

Case Illustration

Anita and Sal (a couple presented in Chapter 8) initially sought counseling for their 6-year-old son Michael, who refused to go to school. Although the parents did not express immediate concern about it, there was a highly conflictual relationship between the eldest daughter, Lauri, age 17, and Anita. The 4-year-old daughter, Pamela, was the joy of the family and carried all the positive family attributes.

Michael was strongly attached to his mother and attentive to her moods and overall happiness. He was defiant toward his father and would often be oppositional to whatever his father wanted from him. When tension developed between father and son, Anita would step in to protect her son and coax him into better behavior. She had given in to many of Michael's demands and did not know how to handle his school refusal.

Lauri was contemptuous of her mother and quickly expressed her feelings that her mother was overly critical, nosy, and demanding. She would turn to her father when she needed permission to spend time with her friends or buy something special, and Anita would be furious when she learned that Sal had responded in a way that she thought was too permissive and indulgent. When Anita tried to reprimand or set limits on her daughter, Lauri would scream at her mother and walk away. Sal would find himself in the middle, trying to calm each one down. Anita was angered by his failure to reprimand Lauri and saw this as further proof of Sal's spoiling his eldest daughter.

Sal and Anita rarely found time to talk about their own relationship or the children, and they would react to each situation as it happened. If Anita tried to express her feelings at a later time, Sal would experience her as critical and demanding, and he would tune out her complaints. In response, Anita would increase her nagging and complaining in the hope that some of it would get through. The couple disagreed about the values and priorities they each set for the children. Sensing that there was no way to work cooperatively, each would try to take control of whatever situation was at hand and make an independent decision. The couple were uncomfortable talking about their relationship and would refocus quickly on the children when questions were asked about their private time and communication unrelated to the children.

The early family sessions focused on getting Michael back to school and helping the parents work out a routine that they could both agree on. Sal's power over Michael was strengthened, and Anita was also helped to set limits that reinforced the objectives set by the parenting team. After this had been accomplished, the focus turned to Lauri and the tension and conflict that centered around mother and daughter. After two sessions with Lauri and her parents, Anita and Sal were asked to come in alone.

Therapist: Last week we talked about Lauri's feelings that she is always being criticized and controlled by Anita. It was strange that most of the time Lauri was talking I could imagine changing her voice and hearing the same words come out of Sal. Except Sal never says how he feels; he just tunes things out or withdraws. Do either of you know what I am talking about?

Sal: (after a lengthy pause) Yeah. I understand exactly why Lauri and Anita can't get along. Anita is too pushy with her.

Anita: Most of it is your fault because you always take her side. If you could only realize that Lauri needs discipline and there shouldn't be two sets of rules to confuse her.

Therapist: (as Sal starts to tune Anita out) Where are you, Sal?

Sal: Huh? Oh, I was just thinking about Lauri.

Therapist: Do you think Anita understood what you were telling me?

Sal: I think I've lost track of where we were.

Therapist: You were telling me how Anita reacts to Lauri in ways that she also acts toward you. I think what just happened was a perfect example. Anita started to lecture you in a way that was pretty strong. There's only one important difference. When Anita does that to Lauri, Lauri screams at her to back off and not be so bossy. When Anita does it to you, you just tune her out. I think that Lauri has to scream twice as loud because she is screaming for you as well as herself. Do you understand what I mean?

Sal: I can see that. I guess Lauri is in the middle. Anita does the same things to me.

Anita: Why does everyone make me out as such a mean person?

Therapist: You are troubled by that.

Anita: I just want what's best for my family.

Therapist: I believe that. You have a great deal of love for your husband and your daughter and you want to make their lives better. When they disagree or just don't listen, you get very upset, and I think we need to look at that more carefully so we can understand it better. You are trying to make things good for the people you love, and you end up feeling like they resent you instead of loving you back or being grateful.

Anita: (starting to cry) Yes, that's what happens. They just don't know how much I love them.

Therapist: Michael seems to be the one who cares about your feelings and how much you need to be loved. Lauri is more like your husband and says "I'm different than you" in ways that you feel are too harsh.

Sal: That's about right.

Therapist: I think what's really going on in this family is that you, Sal, and you, Anita, each would like the other to be different in ways that for one reason or another you can't talk about or change. The kids seem to know what those things are, and they act it out for you. Michael ends up being too close to Anita and angry at Sal. Lauri ends up being too close to Sal and angry at Anita. What needs to happen is that Michael and Lauri need to form their own relationships with both of you instead of being your representatives. That will happen when the two of you can figure out how to work better together for the children's sake and, even more importantly, for the sake of your relationship.

Anita: We don't fight about anything except the children.

Therapist: You don't always fight, but you don't exactly work well together either. Almost every area we have talked about the two of you approach differently. I see that as a potential strength, but for right now it prevents the two of you from working well together.

Anita: I see what you mean. We do see things differently, and we don't always fight, but we never really pull together.

Therapist: I'd like to just work with the two of you for a couple of months. We will of course talk about things that come up with the children, but we'll focus more on how the two of you work together and solve your differences.

Sal: We have put the kids in the middle, and it's not good for anyone. I'm all for it.

Anita and Sal had avoided conflict in their relationship by unknowingly involving the children. The dynamics between them were mirrored in their relationships with their son and elder daughter. Once the parents were able to observe this family pattern, they were easier to approach as a couple with marital problems that needed to be explored. While each was somewhat uncomfortable about the focus on the marriage, they were both highly motivated to correct a situation that was not in the best interest of the children.

Anita and Sal remained in couples treatment for one year. During that time the behavior and school avoidance problems with Michael totally disappeared, and the relationship between Lauri and her mother improved dramatically. This couple would most likely never have sought therapy to improve their marriage or to correct the problematic relationship with their elder daughter. It took Michael's truancy to force the family to admit their need to get help from an outsider. The marriage, although not initially accessible to intervention, proved to be the most effective vehicle for family change.

Involving a Spouse in the Treatment of One Partner's Problem

Psychotherapy is often requested by an individual who is involved in a stressful intimate relationship and who is experiencing distress or psychiatric symptoms that have not previously been defined as related to the relationship. The role of marital dynamics in causing and exacerbating symptoms such as anxiety and depression has been well documented in the literature (Coyne et al. 1987, Dobson et al. 1988, Hafner 1986). While there is not sufficient evidence to suggest that marital treatment is the treatment of choice in all situations, very often psychiatric symptoms are significantly reduced once the problematic marital dynamics are dealt with.

The challenge to the therapist is to engage a spouse who does not wish to be associated with the symptoms and who feels blamed by the therapist's attempts to focus on the marriage. It also can be very difficult to help the symptomatic spouse accept an interpersonal explanation for problems that have been previously defined as purely psychological or physiological.

Timing is an important factor in helping shift the focus from the individual to the couple. If the therapist has developed a good working relationship with the symptomatic spouse, it is less likely that the partner will be able to become involved in marital therapy with the same therapist. It is difficult to establish sufficient therapeutic neutrality to fully engage a partner who feels invited into an existing therapeutic alliance, and it is equally difficult to help the engaged spouse redefine or lose a therapeutic relationship he or she has come to value.

A similar problem is created when one spouse calls to request an individual appointment to discuss a failed or problematic relationship. In the initial telephone contact, the therapist often has to decide whether to accept the request for individual therapy, or to try to make an appointment for the couple to be seen conjointly.

Redefining the focus from individual to marital therapy may appear to pose a risk to the therapist who may fear losing a client entirely should there be resistance against redefining the problem and treatment modality. Challenging an individual to invite a spouse into marital therapy can often jeopardize that person's initial interest and commitment to be in treatment. The therapist, fearing the loss of a potential treatment case, may be reluctant to exert pressure that could cause the individual to look elsewhere for therapy.

The decision to accept or continue individual psychotherapy when the marriage is an important component of the presenting problem may point to ambivalence on the part of the therapist. It is not uncommon for therapists to prefer to work with one spouse because they feel they have better control and expertise in working with individuals. Most professional therapy training is oriented toward the treatment of individuals, and it is not easy for a therapist to develop the confidence and skills necessary to work with couples. For these reasons, an individual claiming his or her spouse is unwilling to participate in marital therapy may be accepted for individual treatment by a therapist who is uncertain about working with the resistance and ambivalent about working with a volatile or conflict-ridden couple. The therapist may rationalize that once the spouse is firmly engaged in therapy, it will be easier to involve the resistant partner.

As Anderson and Stewart (1983) have pointed out, the resistance labeled as existing in one member of a system is rarely located in only that individual. The spouse who claims his or her partner would never attend sessions often carries an equal amount of ambivalence or resistance. In some instances the need to tell the partner that there is a marital problem of sufficient magnitude to warrant professional intervention is too stressful for the unhappy spouse to contemplate. It may be emotionally easier for the spouse to avoid or at least postpone involving an unaware partner.

If the therapist accepts the spouse's explanation that the partner is resistant and decides to proceed with individual therapy, it is unlikely that the partner will ever be able to join sessions in the future. Neutrality will be almost impossible to accomplish, as the partner will usually feel that the therapist is biased toward the spouse who has been in treatment longer. For these reasons the resistance should be thoughtfully explored before the therapist agrees to provide psychotherapy for a problem that is clearly centered in the marital relationship.

Case Illustration

Walter called the therapist for an appointment and said that he was unhappy about his marriage. When the therapist inquired if the couple had been in couples treatment, Walter explained that his wife would probably not agree to see a therapist but that the situation was getting increasingly worse for him.

Therapist: You say the two of you have been drifting apart for a few years.

Walter: Yes. I'm very involved in my job, and she's very caught up in the kids. She's always harping on me to spend more time with the children, but I'm not happy at home any more.

Therapist: I think you did the right thing to want to talk to a therapist, Walter, but I'm not sure that coming in alone from the start is the best plan.

Walter: My wife would never come to a therapist.

Therapist: Well, you know your wife and I don't, so I can't disagree with you, but I wonder if she is also unhappy with the way things are between you.

Walter: I don't think she's aware of how unhappy I am.

Therapist: It sounds like the two of you aren't talking a lot.

Walter: That's about it.

Therapist: You know, Walter, you probably feel like things have gotten so bad no one can help the two of you. Maybe you've already decided to end this relationship and you want help getting out.

Walter: I wouldn't say that exactly. I am pessimistic, and I probably think we can't work it out, but it's not something I know for sure yet.

Therapist: Is there someone else in your life that you care about?

Walter: No. But there could be. I'm attracted to one woman at work, and it could get out of hand pretty quick.

Therapist: Walter, I can sense how bad things are for you. It sounds like your wife isn't paying very much attention to the marriage and you feel pretty much on your own already. But if you need to know for sure if your marriage can be improved, the best way is to come in together from the start. If your wife agrees to come, then you know for sure how important your unhappiness is to her. Maybe she just doesn't see what you're going through and needs to hear from you that you are upset enough to want marital therapy. If she won't come I'll see you alone, but if she does come, even if it's for two or three sessions, then I'll know exactly what you're dealing with. You may not think this will happen, but there is always the chance that your wife might surprise you and tell you that she is also unhappy and wants things to change.

Walter: Well, I'm not optimistic.

Therapist: I will respect whatever decision you make on this. My experience tells me that it's easier to involve your wife in the beginning than it might be if you change your mind down the road. Why don't you just think a bit about our conversation, and make the decision you're most comfortable with? We can go ahead and set up an appointment time.

Walter: My wife doesn't know how I feel. I think it will be hard to tell her.

Therapist: I am sure that's true. It's like starting something that you have probably been thinking about for some time. You started it today by calling me, which was also not easy. The next step may also be hard, but you'll be moving in a way that has got to make things better for you in the long run.

Walter: I'll think about it. Let's set that time up now.

Walter felt neglected and abandoned by his wife but had not confronted her with his feelings. Instead, he had involved himself in work and was vulnerable to starting an affair as a way of replacing his wife entirely. Although Walter felt disconnected from his wife, he was in other ways obviously attached to her and was reluctant to initiate change by introducing the need for marital treatment. To Walter, marital treatment represented divorce. Involving his wife may also have meant perpetuation of a marriage he was closer to ending than he could acknowledge. He also seemed somewhat reluctant to deal with his wife's reaction and the conflict that might develop as part of her response.

Although Walter initially stated that his wife would not come for marital therapy, it was readily apparent that Walter felt uncomfortable confronting his wife and that he possessed a great deal of resistance to inviting her to attend sessions with him.

Ultimately Walter brought his wife to the first session. She had avoided and minimized the problems in their relationship and was frightened to learn the extent of her husband's unhappiness. Walter had indeed set the wheels of change in motion and felt anxious about the future, but he was relieved to end a situation that had become intolerable.

27

The Outcome of Successful Marital Treatment

The theory that is used by the marital therapist shapes the treatment goals and expectations, the interventions, and the criteria that ultimately dictate whether the outcome has been successful. The therapist who focuses on structure is pleased when the structure has been improved and uses this as a guidepost throughout therapy.

Object relations theory encompasses many principles of human behavior and development. It is unfortunate that some of these concepts have been isolated from their broader context and interpreted in ways that misrepresent the overall tenets of the theory (Walsh and Scheinkman 1989).

Object relations theory allows for a focus on emerging identity and ongoing development. The individual is viewed as constantly affected by the earliest internalized self and object representations, but not necessarily doomed to endless repetitions of recorded pathology. Rather, each new relationship and developmental stage provide the opportunity for the discovery of a new facet of self and a reworking of the self in relation to others.

Understanding is the first step in that discovery process. Couples who are locked in destructive projective identification patterns or who can only view themselves in restricted, suffocating ways have fewer options and opportunities to change. Awareness of self-imposed expectations and distortions in how self and others are experienced is a powerful tool to elucidate change and growth.

Many object relations theorists have used the epigenetic principle that development is sequenced in predictable stages. The challenges and needs vary with each stage, and successful outcome is, in part, dependent on the resources and strengths determined by the resolution of previous developmental challenges. Gaps and deficiencies will be carried into subsequent stages and will demand reparation in order that healthy development can proceed.

The purpose of assessing the structure, functions, and content of the representational world is not to label pathology, but to better understand the areas of internalized object relations that are demanding reparation. Until these areas can be approached with new understanding and until long-standing needs are responded to in new ways, mature intimacy and healthy self-esteem remain elusive goals.

The process of completely freeing the self from the invisible chains of the past is not something that can be achieved in months or even years of therapy. It is a process that lasts a lifetime and varies in unpredictable ways according to the unique circumstances and relationships encountered by each individual.

Successful marital therapy is one that has stimulated the partners to experience and comprehend themselves and each other in a new way. Every time spouses are challenged to approach their relationship in a way that liberates them from internalized redundancy, they have made progress. Every time a long-standing deficiency is responded to, the representational world is strengthened, enabling the couple to cope better with the challenges of life.

The therapist who can be part of this discovery process and who can see his or her work in the emergence of a strengthened identity and an enriched relationship has made a vital contribution to the couple's growth and well-being. It is those moments that sustain and inspire those of us who engage in the practice of object relations marital therapy.

References

Adams, D. (1987). Counseling men who batter: a profeminist analysis of five treatment models. In *Feminist Perspectives on Wife Abuse*, ed. M. Bograd and K. Yllo, pp. 1–27. Beverly Hills, CA: Sage.

Akhtar, S., and Byrne, J. (1983). The concept of splitting and its clinical relevance. *American Journal of Psychiatry* 140:1013–1015.

Anderson, C. M., and Stewart, S. (1983). *Mastering Resistance*. New York: Guilford.

Appel, G. (1966). Some aspects of transference and countertransference in marital counselling. *Social Casework* 47:307–312.

Barnett, J. (1966). On cognitive disorders in the obsessional. *Contemporary Psychoanalysis* 2:122–134.

Beavers, W. R. (1985). *Successful Marriage*. New York: W. W. Norton.

Bergman, A. (1982). Considerations about the development of the girl during the separation-individuation process. In *Early Female Development*, ed. D. Mendell, pp. 61–80. New York: Spectrum.

Blum, H. (1987). Countertransference: concepts and controversies. In *Countertransference*, ed. E. Slakter, pp. 87–105. Northvale, NJ: Jason Aronson.

Bowles, D. D. (1988). Development of an ethnic self-concept among blacks. In *Ethnicity and Race: Critical Concepts in Social Work*, ed. C. Jacobs and D. Bowles, pp. 103–113. Washington DC: NASW Press.

Boyd-Franklin, N. (1989). *Black Families in Therapy*. New York: Guilford.

Braverman, S. (1985). One couple, three therapists: therapeutic overdose or collusion breaker? *Journal of Marital and Family Therapy* 11:179–186.

Bromberg, P. M. (1986). The mirror and the mask: on narcissism and psychoanalytic growth. In *Essential Papers on Narcissism*, ed. A. P. Morrison, pp. 438–466. New York: New York University Press.

Chodorow, N. (1974). Family structure and feminine personality. In *Women, Culture and Society*, ed. M. Rolaldo and L. Lamphere, pp. 43–66. Stanford, CA: Stanford University Press.

Coyne, J. C., Kahn, J., and Gotlib, I. H. (1987). Depression. In *Family Interaction and Psychotherapy*, ed. T. Jacob, pp. 509–534. New York: Plenum.

Davis, D. I. (1981). Special problems in family therapy posed by alcohol abuse. In *Family Therapy and Major Psychopathology*, ed. M. R. Lansky, pp. 231–245. New York: Grune & Stratton.

Dicks, H. V. (1963). Object relations theory and marital studies. *British Journal of Medical Psychology* 36:1–12.

Dobson, K. S., Jacobson, N. S., and Victor, J. (1988). Integration of cognitive therapy and behavioral marital therapy. In *Affective Disorders and the Family*, ed. J. Clarkin, G. Haas, and I. D. Glick, pp. 53–88. New York: Guilford.

Eagle, M. N. (1987). The psychoanalytic and the cognitive unconscious. In *Theories of the Unconscious and Theories of the Self*, ed. R. Stern, pp. 155–189. Northvale, NJ: Jason Aronson.

Eichenbaum, L., and Orbach, S. (1983). *Understanding Women: A Feminist Psychoanalytic Approach.* New York: Basic Books.

Erikson, E. H. (1959). *Identity and the Life Cycle.* New York: International Universities Press.

Everett, C., Halperin, S., Volgy, S., and Wissler, A. (1989). *Treating the Borderline Family, A Systemic Approach.* Needham Heights, MA: Allyn and Bacon.

Falicov, C. J. (1992). Love and gender in the Latino marriage. *American Family Therapy Association Newsletter* 48:30–36.

Feldman, L. B. (1982a). Dysfunctional marital conflict. *Journal of Marital and Family Therapy* 8:417–428.

———— (1982b). Sex roles and family dynamics. In *Normal Family Processes*, ed. F. Walsh, pp. 354–379. New York: Guilford.

———— (1986). Sex-role issues in marital therapy. In *Clinical Handbook of Marital Therapy*, ed. N. S. Jacobson and A. S. Gurman, pp. 345–360. New York: Guilford.

———— (1992). *Integrating Individual and Family Therapy.* New York: Brunner/Mazel.

Framo, J. (1970). Symptoms from a family transactional viewpoint. In *Family Therapy in Transition*, ed. N. Ackerman, J. Lieb, and K. Pearce, pp. 125–171. Boston: Little, Brown.

Goldner, V., Penn, P., Sheinberg M., and Walker, G. (1990). Love and violence: gender paradoxes in volatile attachments. *Family Process* 29:343–364.

Goldstein, E. (1984). *Ego Psychology and Social Work Treatment.* New York: The Free Press.

———— (1990). *Borderline Disorders: Clinical Models and Techniques.* New York: Guilford.

Hafner, R. J. (1986). *Marriage and Mental Illness: A Sex Roles Perspective.* New York: Guilford.

Hamilton, N. G. (1988). *Self and Others: Object Relations Theory in Practice.* Northvale, NJ: Jason Aronson.

Heiss, J. (1981). Social roles. In *Social Psychology,* ed. M. Rosenberg and R. H. Turner, pp. 94–128. New York: Basic Books.

Horner, A. J. (1987). The unconscious and the archaeology of human relationships. In *Theories of the Unconscious and Theories of the Self,* ed. R. Stern, pp. 27–43. Hillsdale, NJ: The Analytic Press.

———— (1989). *Object Relations and the Developing Ego in Therapy.* Rev. and exp. ed. Northvale, NJ: Jason Aronson.

Jacobson, E. (1964). *The Self and the Object World.* New York: International Universities Press.

Joseph, B. (1987). Projective identification: clinical aspects. In *Projection, Identification and Projective Identification,* ed. J. Sandler, pp. 65–76. Madison, CT: International Universities Press.

Kantor, D., and Kupferman, W. (1985). The client's interview of the therapist. *Journal of Marriage and Family Therapy* 11:225–244.

Kernberg, O. F. (1965). Notes on countertransference. *Journal of the American Psychoanalytic Association* 13:38–56.

———— (1972). Early ego integration and object relations. *Annals of the New York Academy of Sciences* 193:233–246.

———— (1975). *Borderline Conditions and Pathological Narcissism.* New York: Jason Aronson.

———— (1985). Normal narcissism in middle age. In *Internal World and External Reality,* pp. 121–134. New York: Jason Aronson.

———— (1987a). Projection and projective identification: developmental and clinical aspects. In *Projection, Identification, Projective Identification,* ed. J. Sandler, pp. 93–115. Madison, CT: International Universities Press.

———— (1987b). The dynamic unconscious. In *Theories of the Unconscious and Theories of the Self,* ed. R. Stern, pp. 3–26. Hillsdale, NJ: The Analytic Press.

Kohut, H. (1971). *The Analysis of the Self.* New York: International Universities Press.

———— (1977). *The Restoration of the Self.* New York: International Universities Press.

Lansky, M. R. (1981a). Treatment of the narcissistically vulnerable couple. In *Family Therapy and Major Psychopathology*, pp. 163–182. New York: Grune & Stratton.

———— (1981b). Family psychotherapy in the hospital. In *Family Psychotherapy and Major Psychopathology*, pp. 395–414. New York: Grune & Stratton.

Lax, R., Bach, S., and Burland, J. A., eds. (1986). *Self and Object Constancy.* New York: Guilford.

Levinson, V., and Ashenberg Straussner, L. A. (1978). Social workers as enablers in the treatment of alcoholics. *Social Casework* 59:14–20.

Luepnitz, D. A. (1988). *The Family Interpreted.* New York: Basic Books.

Mack, R. N. (1989). Spouse abuse—a dyadic approach. In *Treating Couples*, ed. G. R. Weeks, pp. 191–214. New York: Brunner/Mazel.

Mahler, M. (1975). *The Psychological Birth of the Human Infant.* New York: Basic Books.

McDevitt, J. B., and Mahler, M. S. (1986). Object constancy, individuality and internalization. In *Self and Object Constancy*, ed. R. F. Lax, S. Bach, and J. Burland, pp. 11–28. New York: Guilford.

McGoldrick, M. (1982). Normal families: an ethnic perspective. In *Normal Family Processes*, ed. F. Walsh, pp. 399–420. New York: Guilford.

McGoldrick, M., Anderson, C. M., and Walsh, F. (1989). *Women in Families.* New York: W. W. Norton.

McGoldrick, M., and Preto, N. (1984). Ethnicity and marriage. *Family Process* 23:347–361.

Meissner, W. W. (1978). The conceptualization of marriage and family dynamics from a psychoanalytic perspective. In *Marriage and Marital Therapy*, ed. J. J. Paolino and B. S. McCrady, pp. 25–88. New York: Brunner/Mazel.

——— (1980). The problem of internalization and structure formation. *International Journal of Psycho-Analysis* 61:237–247.

——— (1982). Notes toward a psychoanalytic theory of marital and family dynamics. *International Journal of Family Psychiatry* 3:189–207.

——— (1986a). The earliest internalizations. In *Self and Object Constancy*, ed. R. Lax and S. Bach, pp. 29–72. New York: Guilford.

——— (1986b). *Psychotherapy and the Paranoid Process*. Northvale, NJ: Jason Aronson.

——— (1987). Projection and projective identification. In *Projection and Projective Identification*, ed. J. Sandler, pp. 27–49. Madison, CT: International Universities Press.

Miller, A. (1981). *Prisoners of Childhood*. New York: Basic Books.

Moultrup, D. J. (1990). *Husbands, Wives and Lovers*. New York: Guilford.

Nichols, W. C. (1988). *Marital Therapy: An Integrative Approach*. New York: Guilford.

Norton, D. G. (1983). Black family life patterns, the development of self and cognitive development of black children. In *The Psychosocial Development of Minority Group Children*, pp. 182–193. New York: Brunner/Mazel.

Ogden, T. (1987). On projective identification. *International Journal of Psycho-Analysis* 60:357–373.

Porder, M. (1987). Projective identification: an alternative hypothesis. *Psychoanalytic Quarterly* 56:431–451.

Ray, M. H. (1986). Phenomenology of failed object constancy. In *Self and Object Constancy*, ed. R. Lax, S. Bach, and J. A. Burland, pp. 233–250. New York: Guilford.

Richter, H. (1974). *The Family as Patient*. New York: Farrar, Strauss & Giroux.

Riley, M. W. (1978). Aging, social change and the power of ideas. *Daedalus* 107:39–52.

Rockland, L. (1989). *Supportive Therapy*. New York: Basic Books.

Rosen, H. (1985). *Piagetian Dimensions of Clinical Relevance*. New York: Columbia University Press.

Rosenbaum, A., and O'Leary, K. D. (1986). The treatment of marital violence. In *Clinical Handbook of Marital Therapy*, ed. N. S. Jacobson and A. S. Gurman, pp. 385–406. New York: Guilford.

Sandler, J., and Rosenblatt, B. (1962). The concept of the representational world. *Psychoanalytic Study of the Child* 17:128–162. New York: International Universities Press.

Scharff, D., and Scharff, J. S. (1987). *Object Relations Family Therapy*. Northvale, NJ: Jason Aronson.

———— (1991). *Object Relations Couple Therapy*. Northvale, NJ: Jason Aronson.

Scharff, J. S., ed. (1989). *Foundations of Object Relations Family Therapy*. Northvale, NJ: Jason Aronson.

Schwartzman, M. S. (1984). Narcissistic transferences: implications for the treatment of couples. *Dynamic Psychotherapy* 2:5–17.

Schwoeri, L., and Schwoeri, F. (1981). Family therapy of borderline patients: diagnostic and treatment issues. *International Journal of Family Psychiatry* 2:237–250.

———— (1982). Interactional and intrapsychic dynamics in a family with a borderline patient. *Psychotherapy Theory, Research and Practice* 19:198–204.

Seinfeld, J. (1990). *The Bad Object*. Northvale, NJ: Jason Aronson.

Shapiro, E. R., Shapiro, R. L., Zinner, J., and Berkowitz, D. (1977). The borderline ego and the working alliance: implications for family and individual treatment. *International Journal of Psycho-Analysis* 58:77–87.

Sharpe, S. A. (1990). The oppositional couple: a developmental object relations approach to diagnosis and treatment. In *New Dimensions in Adult Development*, ed. R. A. Nemiroff and C. A. Colarusso, pp. 386–415. New York: Basic Books.

Siegel, J. (1991). Analysis of projective identification: an object relations approach to marital treatment. *Journal of Clinical Social Work* 19:71–81.

———— (1992). Object relations marital therapy: engaging the couple. In *Case Studies in Social Work Practice*, ed. C. LeCroy, pp. 22–27. Belmont, CA: Wadsworth Press.

Singer-Magdoff, L. J. (1990). Early fit and faulty fit: object relations in marital therapy. In *When One Wants Out and the Other Doesn't*, ed. J. F. Crosby, pp. 118–135. New York: Brunner/Mazel.

Skynner, R. (1987). *Explorations with Families*. Ed. J. R. Schlapobersky. New York: Routledge.

Slipp, S. (1984). *Object Relations: A Dynamic Bridge Between Individual and Family Treatment*. New York: Jason Aronson.

———— (1988). *The Technique and Practice of Object Relations Family Therapy*. Northvale, NJ: Jason Aronson.

Solomon, M. F. (1985). Treatment of narcissistic and borderline disorders in marital therapy: suggestions toward an enhanced therapeutic approach. *Clinical Social Work* 13:141–156.

———— (1989). *Narcissism and Intimacy: Love and Marriage in an Age of Confusion*. New York: W. W. Norton.

Stein, H. F. (1984). The problem of cultural persistence, and the differentiation of self in one's culture. In *The Best of the Family: Compendium Two*, ed. E. Pendagast, pp. 85–94. New Rochelle, NY: Center for Family Learning.

Stern, D. (1985). *The Interpersonal World of the Infant*. New York: Basic Books.

Stewart, R. H., Peters, T. C., Marsh, S., and Peters, M. J. (1975). An object relations approach to psychotherapy with marital couples, families and children. *Family Process* 14:161–172.

Stierlin, H., and Weber, G. (1989). *Unlocking the Family Door*. New York: Brunner/Mazel.

Stolorow, R. D. (1975). The narcissistic function of masochism (and sadism). *International Journal of Psycho-Analysis* 56:441–448.

Stolorow, R. D., and Atwood, G. E. (1987). From the subjectivity of science to a science of subjectivity. In *Theories of the Unconscious and Theories of the Self*, ed. R. Stern, pp. 213–220. Northvale, NJ: Jason Aronson.

Strothman, L. J. (1985). Early developmental processes and adult intimate violence. In *Yearbook of Psychoanalysis and Psychotherapy*, ed. R. Langs, vol. 1, pp. 77–118. Emerson, NJ: New Concept Press.

Swidler, A. (1971). Love and adulthood in American culture. In *Family in Transition*, ed. A. Skolnick and J. Skolnick, pp. 286–305. Boston: Little, Brown.

Tansey, M. J., and Burke, W. F. (1989). *Understanding Countertransference*. Hillsdale, NJ: The Analytic Press.

Tevlin, H., and Leiblum, S. R. (1983). Sex-role stereotypes and female sexual dysfunction. In *The Stereotyping of Women*, ed. J. Franks and E. Rothblum, pp. 129–151. New York: Springer.

Tolpin, M., and Kohut, H. (1980). The disorders of the self: the psychopathology of the first years of life. In *The Course of Life: Psychoanalytic Contributions toward Understanding Personality Development*, vol. 1, ed. S. Greenspan and G. Pollock, pp. 425–442. Washington, DC: National Institute of Mental Health.

Volkan, V. (1976). *Primitive Internalized Object Relations*. New York: International Universities Press.

———— (1979). *Cyprus—War and Adaptation: A Psychoanalytic History of Two Ethnic Groups in Conflict*. Charlottesville: University Press of Virginia.

———— (1981). Transference and countertransference. In *Object and Self: A Developmental Approach*, ed. S. Tuthman, C. Kaye, and M. Zimmerman, pp. 429–451. New York: International Universities Press.

Walrond-Skinner, S. (1977). *Family Therapy: The Treatment of Natural Systems*. Boston: Routledge & Kegan.

Walsh, F., and Scheinkman, M. (1989). (Fe)male: the hidden gender dimension in models of family therapy. In *Women in Families*, ed. M. McGoldrick, C. Anderson, and F. Walsh, pp. 16–41. New York: W. W. Norton.

White, M. T. (1986). Self constancy: the elusive concept. In *Self and Object Constancy*, ed. R. Lax, S. Bach, and J. A. Burland, pp. 73–94. New York: Guilford.

Winston, A., Pinsker, H., and McCullough, L. (1986). A review of supportive psychotherapy. *Hospital and Community Psychiatry* 37:1105–1114.

Winnicott, D. W. (1958). The capacity to be alone. In *The Maturational Processes and the Facilitating Environment*, pp. 29–36. New York: International Universities Press, 1965.

———— (1962). Ego integration in child development. In *The Maturational Processes and The Facilitating Environment*, pp. 56–63. New York: International Universities Press, 1965.

Zinner, J., and Shapiro, R. (1972). Projective identification as a mode of perception and behavior in families of adolescents. *International Journal of Psycho-Analysis* 53:523–530.

———— (1975). Splitting in families of borderline adolescents. In *Borderline States in Psychiatry*, ed. J. Mack, pp. 103–122. New York: Grune & Stratton.

Index